MEN OF KENT

MEN OF KENT

TEN BOYS, A FAST BOAT, AND THE COACH WHO MADE THEM CHAMPIONS

RICK RINEHART

LYONS PRESS
GUILFORD, CONNECTICUT

An imprint of Globe Pequot Press

Lyons Press is an imprint of Globe Pequot Press.

Project editor: David Legere
Text design: Sheryl Kober
Layout artist: Kevin Mak

Library of Congress Cataloging-in-Publication Data is available on file.

ISBN 978-1-59921-932-5

Printed in United States of America

10 9 8 7 6 5 4 3 2 1

FOR THE MEN AND WOMEN
OF KENT SCHOOL

There are only two ways to live your life. One is as though nothing is a miracle. The other is as though everything is a miracle.

—ALBERT EINSTEIN

CONTENTS

A NOTE ON THE TEXT

Because *Men of Kent* is intended for a broad audience and not just followers of the sport of rowing, I have provided a glossary of rowing terms as the appendix to this book. While I have done my best to limit the jargon that surrounds the sport, it didn't always work to interrupt the narrative to explain some arcane detail. I hope that the glossary will be useful to those to whom I've thrown a terminological curve. Similarly, I've used English and American terms for high school rankings pretty much interchangeably, but for those unfamiliar with the English educational system, they parallel American grades as follows: Third formers are freshmen; fourth formers, sophomores; fifth formers, juniors; and sixth formers, seniors.

Finally, a word or two on the title of this book. The original "Men of Kent" were said to have been brave warriors who rebelled (albeit unsuccessfully) against William the Conqueror's usurpation of the English crown in 1066. Pilgrims known collectively as Men of Kent (because they were descended from the rebels) settled Scituate, Massachusetts, in 1625 and were known for their boatbuilding skills and prowess on the sea. For a while a launch named *Men of Kent* plied the waters at Henley, but it is unknown whether this was a gesture toward the first American boarding school to compete at the regatta or for the martyrs of 1066.

PROLOGUE: HOME RIVER

Advancing spring, pervasive and serene,
Assuaged the river with calmer powers . . .
While on its surface, smooth as a machine,
The first shell cut the water, and the rowers
With unphrased happiness at spring returning
Strained to the rhythmic pull, their long oars churning
—ROBERT S. HILLYER, "AN ODE"

The Housatonic River in Connecticut is borne of a web of smaller rivers and tributaries in neighboring New York and Massachusetts, many of which became waterways for pollutants from the dawning of the Industrial Revolution to the Superfund cleanups of recent years. Still, in northwestern Connecticut the river has a wild and hearty look to it; rapids yield to reaches, dams, and rapids again as the broad stream cuts its way through the Berkshire foothills. Right below one such rapid on the east bank of the river lies the town of Kent, at one time a sleepy New England village that seemed a day's drive from everything; now a bustling, hip, and pricey place that feels like just another distant suburb of New York. As the rapid yields to flat water at the Route 341 bridge, a clapboard-sided monster rises on the river's west bank, later followed by a larger cluster of handsome Georgian buildings linked by straight, purposeful pathways under a canopy of maple and elm trees. The redbrick buildings are the nucleus of the Kent School campus; the freshly painted, wood-sided structure by the river is the school's newly constructed, $2.1 million rowing center, a three-level homage to a centuries-old sport, some of whose greatest races have been rowed within fifty miles of the site. The Housatonic drifts by passively, pushing onward toward the Long Island Sound, passing the Yale boathouse at Derby, and taking with it such memories as a body of water can hold for an oarsman whose last race is now three decades gone.

———

It had been a while since I'd been to Kent the spring morning I drove up to meet with the current headmaster, Dick Schell, and the head of the English Department, Joan Beattie, to discuss a book project for the school's upcoming centennial. I hadn't been able to give much to Kent over the years; $100 here or there, maybe, but certainly nothing that would merit a building or even so much as a brick in my name. Dick had kindly agreed to officiate at my wedding in Colorado in 2003—he was Kent class of 1969, and a longtime friend of my family's—and it was at the reception that I proposed the idea of a book to celebrate Kent's centennial. I further offered my services pro bono; if there was anything I could do, it was make a book, and if I could do one for Kent it would help to absolve years of guilt for not doing something meaningful for the school that had done so much for me. Dick took up the idea immediately, e-mails were exchanged, and I scheduled a side trip to Kent following one of my business trips to New York. I was both apprehensive and excited about returning to the place: excited to be revisiting the pastel beauty of a Litchfield County spring, apprehensive about how much of the past I would be pulled back into. I had, after all, made the West my home for over three decades, and Kent was not the kind of place that figured into the context of my adopted lifestyle. (Indeed, ask any Coloradan for his or her idea of a boarding school, and inevitably the paradigm offered will be Harry Potter's cartoonish Hogwarts.) Not surprisingly, few friendships from my Kent years had overcome the challenging triad of geographical, temporal, and emotional distance, though in the background of my daily ruminations on matters past and present, nine boys and their inspirational mentor occupy an enduring, and pleasingly gentle, place.

I decided to drive to the school by a familiar route, from the south along Route 7 up the western side of Connecticut, as I had so many times in the past. Although I knew it might be painful, I wanted to see what had changed in thirty-three years. Once beyond New Milford, as it turns out, much appeared to be the same. When I got to the village of Gaylordsville, I was startled to see that a place called the Basket Shop was still in operation, a sight that brought forward the most melancholic of recollections, that of love long gone. Three decades earlier it had been a refuge for me and the girl to whom I was inseparably attached for two years and nearly married; the owners, friends of her parents, would pull us out of school for a few hours on the weekends to hang out at the store. We did little of that—we usually retreated to the attic, our Room at the Top, where the owners would conveniently forget about us until it was time to return to school.

By the time I reached the somewhat more cheerful Bulls Bridge Tavern a few miles north of the Basket Shop, however, I had reminded myself of why it didn't work out with the girl, and had taken myself to task for stumbling into such a sentimental tar pit. (Alas, she was not to be my Simone Signoret, nor I her Laurence Harvey.)

At Bulls Bridge the Housatonic also rises to meet you as its flat, broad water pools behind a dam. Anglers who have a certain affection for a spot will often refer to it as their "home river"; here, where the Housatonic first becomes rowable as you head north along Route 7, was for one unforgettable season my home river. From this point to the Route 341 bridge, the river would be clogged with crews on spring afternoons, coxswains barking stroke counts like randomly scattered seals commanding an estuary. A little farther along is the finish line to the Kent racecourse, poorly marked now on the west bank of the river. Because the course was changed from a mile to 1,500 meters in length the year after I left Kent, I had to keep an eye on the odometer to find the old starting line upriver. But all else was familiar—every bend, eddy, and riffle.

As the river broadened, my mind beheld a familiar idyll, once again recalling the smoky dawn of some early spring morning so many years ago and the sound of eight oars hitting their locks, their metronomic cadence pulling sixty feet of cedar along on flat water. In this musing oar blades strike the water and are pulled through to a clean exit, the bow rises slightly, and eight small whirlpools race away from the boat, looking like so many feathers spinning on glass. The coxswain's muted commands bounce off the surrounding hills in the stillness of the dawn; light filters through mist to cast the oarsmen in a divine glow. Trailing the shell is a small powerboat in which a stooped figure at the stern just sits and observes as an artist contemplates his next brushstroke. "Moving well," he ultimately tells the crew, with no further instruction. The image is an occasional visitor to my consciousness, that gentle place that is there when I need to exit the chaos of life for a moment or two.

My reverie was soon broken as road and river separated about a mile from the town of Kent. Here, vestiges of old farmsteads that must have been the core of the village's early economy dot the broad valley, all in stark contrast to the new McMansions rising in their midst that drive the local economy in a different way now—mostly through retail shopping and real estate, from what I can observe. Because they were one of the first prominent couples to move to the Kent area in the late 1970s, I decide to blame former secretary of state Henry Kissinger and his wife for this, but mostly because I want to and not because there is any evidence that they were the intentional vanguard of the arrival of the Beautiful People in the valley. Kent's secret wasn't going to be kept forever, and I remind myself that it must be the height of some sort of arrogance to assert the superiority of the past over the present.

Once in Kent I was on automatic pilot: left at the monument that marks the turn on to Route 341, over the bridge, and just like that the Kent campus presented itself. Except for bumping into the imposing new rowing center on the north side of 341, I could probably still walk the place blindfolded. I parked the car in the main lot by the Science Building and struck out for the headmaster's office like a third former summoned to explain a bad math grade or an ill-timed, ill-advised water balloon.

As my experience at the Basket Shop demonstrated, one never likes to revisit one's old haunts only to have them trigger an unwelcome, sodden emotion. Happily, the Kent campus looked even better than it had in my most embellished recollection of the place; though school was no longer in session for the year, workers buzzed about, fussing over a flower garden here and a loose paving stone there. Kent, which had been coed since the 1960s but had exiled its girls until 1986 to a mountaintop campus five miles away, had added several new buildings since my era to accommodate the transition to a completely coed institution. Thus new dorms had been built for the girls, and the old facilities had been upgraded and expanded, all without compromising the architectural harmony of the original campus. In fact, the additions only improved it. The place looked fabulous, making the Kent of my time seem like a discounted knockoff of what I now beheld. Its discreet modernity mocked nostalgia for the Spartan conditions of a poorer Kent, a Kent whose pride in frugality, while virtuous, nearly brough it to ruin.

Dick Schell being a man with a mind of the proverbial steel trap, we got through our meeting quickly and efficiently. After catching up on family news briefly, I prepared to leave, but I wasn't quite ready to leave Kent yet. I knew I was there for another reason, a reason that lay in that new behemoth of a building by the river. Somewhere in there glowed a talisman—a touchstone that would link me with the past and serve as proof positive that I was part of something extraordinary once. I wasn't looking for anything obvious like a trophy case or a photograph; it had to be something few others would remember, and to somehow stumble across it would verify that I hadn't made it all up, that it hadn't been the stuff of some poorly concocted war story. I turned to Dick. "Can I see the rowing center?"

Dick cheerfully obliged me, and before I got there a custodian had already opened up the place and departed. I entered the building on the first floor through a side door that opened to a hallway, off of which were two rather pedestrian-looking offices. Though scarcely a month old, the offices already looked well used, with papers strewn about and desk chairs askew. Coaches' offices. At the end of the hall, I turned right and entered a somewhat grander chamber containing trophy cases, photographs, and other memorabilia, its wood-paneled walls, fine furniture, and carpet clearly suggesting shrine. Wanting to take in the full sweep of the place before absorbing the details, I ignored the trophy cases for the moment and moved on to an impressive room containing spanking-new rowing practice tanks. A sign and a photograph told me that this room was named for retired coach William Hartwell Perry Jr. The Boss. Nice touch. Thanks to whoever thought of that.

I found a stairway and headed up to the second floor, which was all business: rowing machines, ergometers, weights—everything an oarsman or -woman would want as the ice still held the Housatonic. There was only one ornament in the room, but it was nevertheless large and imposing: an upside-down eight-oared shell hanging from the ceiling, oars in locks. It was an old one from the end of the wood boat era, but it appeared to be in excellent condition. I walked to the bow to see which one it was, and when I saw that it was the *Frederick Herbert Sill*—my 60 feet of cedar—my heart didn't stop so much as rise. Wooden boats normally don't hold up this well over the years, unless someone has intentionally taken them out of commission early. After being made obsolete and replaced by the next generation of rowing shells, boats at Kent were normally sent down to the clubs for use, where neophyte oarsmen and coxswains tended to inflict some unintentional wear and tear. Someone had made it a point to preserve the *Sill*, and I was grateful for that.

Leaving the second floor my eye caught the outline of a familiar photograph hanging on a wall, nine boys in blue warm-ups hoisting a trophy against the steel-gray sky of a stormy afternoon long ago. The caption simply read 1972: NATIONAL SCHOOLBOY CHAMPIONS. Standing at the back of the photograph was a tall, beaming, eighteen-year-old that I hardly recognized. ("Can't be me," I teased myself. "He has *hair*.") I smiled, but neither the photograph nor the *Sill* was what I came to the Rowing Center to find.

I returned to the big room on the first floor. Now I examined the various artifacts and memorabilia in more detail, finding yet another photograph from 1972 among a suite of pictures depicting Kent Henley crews over the years. I moved over to a display case that held some familiar Kent rowing iconography, such as the *Life* magazine cover story on the 1948 crew; a letter from President Franklin Roosevelt wishing some crew from the 1930s good luck at Henley; and a congratulatory letter from President Richard Nixon to the 1972 crew. All were items that I had been aware of from flipping through scrapbooks during my years at Kent, but it was satisfying to know that they now had a more or less permanent home. I walked over to yet another display case, this one containing items that were not as familiar to me, but should have been, because it held items contributed by members of the 1972 crew. Among them was an oath I had signed for the Stewards of the Henley Royal Regatta; my atavistic, teenage signature mesmerized me for a moment before my eyes drifted to another level of the case.

And in a flash of red, there it was.

I'll be damned, I cursed to myself. Here was the connection I was looking for, a simple artifact not so much deliberately saved as not summarily tossed out after thirty-odd years. We acquire and then dispose of so many things over time: Why is it that certain, otherwise perfectly mundane objects are suddenly pulled out of the yard sale or saved from the trash and returned to the storage bin? Why do I still have the shirts taken off the backs of vanquished oarsmen from three decades ago, notwithstanding my wife's attempts to turn them into cleaning rags? I suppose it's the same reason our grown son's Cub Scout uniform still hangs in the closet; though let go we must, a part of us still clings to the perceived innocence of an earlier time, when the world seemed to be a gentler place, though in our heart of hearts we know that it was anything but. It was we who were the innocents—blindly believing that our virtue would make the world a better place, that faith and grace would be all we needed to get by, that if we just believed in ourselves we could accomplish almost anything.

How unfamiliar those boys look now.

"Life," the late novelist John Cheever wrote in *The Wapshot Chronicles*, "is a mysterious gift." For a white Christian male conveniently born between major wars and the good luck to avoid a minor one, life is the gift that keeps on giving. Although I do not believe that there are any true entitlements in the world—being born into a wealthy family only means that you hold the winning lottery ticket—I was fortunate to grow up with a modicum of security, the Cold War being the only dark cloud steadily looming over the landscape of our otherwise cheerful existence. My parents were by no means rich and chose to bide their time until this or that inheritance came through from my successful grandparents; my mother stayed at home and took care of us, as mothers did then, and my father did as he pleased, which was to teach writing, play his music, and drive around town in his 1948 Chevrolet convertible coupe. We only rose above our middle-class status when it came to education; my grandparents footed the bill for private school—modest lottery winnings—which ultimately got my sister and me to Kent and my brother to Exeter. Beyond that, everything else we wanted to have or do was more or less up to us.

Unlike preceding generations, there were no guarantees of a place at Harvard or a position in the family firm, much less an undeserved crack at some varsity squad as a favor to a significant benefactor. Not only did our parents see to it, in a rebellious sort of way, that these things would never come to us, they were also swept up in the social movements of the 1960s and 1970s, whose crucible was a level playing field. This attitude ultimately granted me the freedom to drop out of college three times, lead a nomadic existence for a time, and try new things I had no business doing. If I failed, only I would suffer the consequences. If I succeeded, it was on to the bonus round. As it turned out, this was a gift that I could not have asked for in my wildest dreams.

And so it was that I approached the sport of rowing, when, in 1972, I just happened to be the lucky square peg in a situation where a round one wouldn't do. What happened afterward was so outside the normal course of my life that even today I recall it with all the confidence of a half-remembered dream. But I had some help, nine boys crossing the threshold of manhood with me as one breathlessly achieves the first Henley course marker appropriately known as the Barrier. With little experience and generally unexceptional athletic ability, we somehow rowed as though we didn't know what it was like to lose—indeed, I retired from the sport resting on the improbable laurels of never having lost an official race over three years of rowing. Far better oarsmen, several on the 1972 boat, lived through the ignominy of a failed season, most notably that of 1971, for which hopes had been high. Following that debacle, 1972 was viewed well south of even a "rebuilding year"; a winning record didn't seem improbable so much as impossible. But after Coach Hart Perry had decided on his crew from bow to stern, it was as if we had become captives of a mysterious agency of power—"chemistry," to use the trite but true expression, but still an obscure enough notion to make you wonder just where in blazes it had come from, and why.

And all this was our foreground to an improbable context—the year that prophesied chaos, 1972, the Year of the Rat in the Vietnamese zodiac. We were still at war then, and as easily as I found myself drifting the salubrious waters of the Thames that summer, I well could have been in an Army boot camp, save for that good fortune. We first heard about the Watergate break-in that June in the *London Times* and on the BBC; we were cautioned to stay away from Northern Ireland after the outbreak of sectarian violence there following Bloody Sunday the preceding January. It was the year that bridged the Age of Aquarius to the era of big hair, leisure suits, disco, and decadence—a blight on the cultural landscape otherwise known as the 1970s. It was the year that eleven amateur athletes were murdered by Palestinian terrorists at the Munich Olympics.

But all such pivotal years have their prolegomena, and those for 1972 extend back nearly twenty years. Indeed, to understand 1972—both the times and the small story I was a part of—one must first understand 1953.

I
1953

The best thing about the past is that it's over.

—John Gimlette

As far as the people of Britain were concerned, New Year's Day 1953 couldn't have come a moment too soon.

Though seven years from victory in World War II, 1952 may have been the nadir of postwar Britain's slip into economic austerity and general cheerlessness. This was no better demonstrated than in the government's ongoing regulation of textiles, which confined clothing stores to "'utility' products . . . usually of extreme drabness reminiscent of Eastern Europe," according to historian Kenneth Morgan in his book *Britain Since 1945*. Furthermore, "many women wore headscarves reminiscent of Balkan peasants; not the least of them were the royal princesses, Elizabeth and Margaret Rose." Though food rationing on certain products was gradually being lifted, Britons had to endure nearly another full year of rationing of their beloved tea, an indignity if there ever was one. Even holiday spots were crowded and glamourless and accessible only by standing room–only prewar rail cars.

Beginning with the death of the popular yet "ordinary," as he was viewed by many, King George VI on February 5, the year 1952 marked the end of what one historian has called "a great age," whose neo-athletic ideals included "esprit de corps, self-control, dignity, tireless effort, fair play, and discipline."

The year also saw the second-worst rail accident in Britain's history, when on October 6 a London-bound express train plowed into a stationary local train, which further caused a third train to crash. One hundred and twelve people perished in the wrecks. The year ended ignominiously with the Great Smog befalling London from December 5 to December 9, a catastrophe that may have been a catalyst for the modern environmental movement. A cold fog had descended upon the city, prompting Londoners to burn more coal than normal. Furthermore, London had just replaced the last of its electric trams with diesel buses, rendering the ground-based atmosphere into a nasty cocktail of pollutants. Visibility suffered as well; driving was impossible at times, and even theaters had to cancel events because audiences couldn't see the stage. Many who had preexisting respiratory problems died within a few days; over the next several months it is estimated that the Great Smog was responsible for some 8,000 deaths.

Nineteen fifty-two also proved to be something of a low point for Britain's athletes. Highly touted distance runner Roger Bannister—arguably the fastest man in the world at the time—had been favored to not only win the 1500 meters at the Summer Olympics but also set a new world record for the race. An exhausted Bannister finished fourth instead, much to the embarrassment of his countrymen, and in a collapse that came to symbolize Great Britain's performance as a whole at the Helsinki Olympics. In an outcome that might have been scripted for a Monty Python skit, Britain's only gold medal came in an equestrian event that finished just eight minutes before the official close of the 1952 Summer Olympics. Britain also failed to medal in the sport it had nurtured and elevated to elite status, rowing, having been dominated by crews from the United States and Europe as well as a new upstart in the sport, the Soviet Union. Only a near sweep of trophies at the Henley Royal Regatta the preceding July had prevented English crews from further embarrassment in international competition.

But by early 1953 things started to turn around for Britain. Tea rationing had been lifted, and soon to follow were the elimination of similar restrictions on the sale of sweets and sugar as well as petrol. English science was restored to prominence when Francis Crick, together with American James D. Watson, announced that they had determined the chemical structure of DNA on February 28. The English male regained his swagger with the debut of an iconic protagonist whose appeal continues unabated in film to this day: On April 23 James Bond, Agent 007, made his first appearance in Ian Fleming's novel *Casino Royale*. On May 29 Sir Edmund Hillary and his Sherpa, Tenzing Norgay, topped Mount Everest, the first successful human ascent of the mountain. Even Roger Bannister had returned to form, posting a 4:02 mile at a track meet on June 27—the third-fastest mile ever—positioning him to make a serious attempt to be the first human to run a mile in less than four minutes. And English crews had once again dominated the Henley Royal Regatta, winning eight of ten events.

But the occasion that most Britons will forever remember 1953 by was the coronation of their new queen in June of that year. As much as the death of King George VI had cast the nation in gloom for much of the preceding year, anticipation of the coronation of his elder daughter had Brits positively giddy with excitement. Unlike the bespectacled, dowdy matron with the mechanical hand wave so lampooned today, the younger Elizabeth II was known for her vitality, sense of adventure, and willingness to reach out to not only her own countrymen but to all citizens of the Commonwealth of Nations as well. During World War II she became the first female member of the Royal Family to serve on active duty in the armed forces, driving a truck for what was known as the Women's Auxiliary Territorial Service. (Indeed, so valuable did she regard her training with the "common" women of the service that the future queen would break with tradition and send her four children away to school rather than have them privately tutored.) She and her sister, Margaret, had scandalously snuck out of Buckingham Palace to revel with celebratory crowds after midnight the day the war in Europe ended. A year later she visited the Henley Royal Regatta for the first time, which after a wartime hiatus had resumed competition with a brand-new, eight-oared event for English schoolboys under the age of nineteen. With her permission, the event, which would be opened to international competition in 1964, would henceforth be known as the Princess Elizabeth Challenge Cup.

Befitting a queen crowned on the eve of a technological revolution, Elizabeth II's coronation on June 2, 1953, was broadcast on live television in Britain, France, Holland, and Germany and shown roughly twelve hours later in the United States and Canada. Because a satellite in space off of which to bounce a TV signal wouldn't be available for another nine years, "telerecordings" of the coronation were flown to North America in three stages by Canberra jet bombers. The feed for NBC and ABC came from Montreal via Buffalo, while CBS arranged for a Canberra to drop off its telerecording directly in New York.

No doubt watching from her apartment in Manhattan on June 3 was a twenty-one-year-old mother pregnant with her second child, though the fine late-spring weather may have been a temptation for a trip to the park with her toddling daughter of two. *Thank goodness,* she might have thought, *George is no longer traveling and can help out a bit more when the baby comes.* The Korean War seemed to be winding down as well, relieving her of worry that her husband might be drafted into the Army. Buried in the back pages of the *New York Times,* though, was word that President Eisenhower had recently committed $1 billion in aid and 300,000 small arms to help the French thwart a

Communist takeover of Vietnam. Eisenhower was careful to emphasize that no U.S. troops would be committed to the conflict. At least not for now.

———

Meanwhile, 200 miles away in Hanover, New Hampshire, a Dartmouth junior was looking back on a just-completed rowing season that would inform the rest of his life.

William Hartwell Perry Jr. first sat in a racing boat "under the watchful eye of Rod Beebe Sr." in 1945 while at summer camp at Tabor Academy. Still, when he later attended Noble and Greenough School in Dedham, Massachusetts, he chose baseball over rowing his eighth-grade year. Striking out "more than everybody else put together" on the fourth team, as Perry recollects, he was gently asked by his coach, gesturing toward the school's boathouse, if he would "consider another sport." Young Perry took the hint and over the next four years rose through the club ranks to make the varsity four by the time he was a senior, having what he later referred to as a pretty good year. Two of his fellow oarsmen would go on to distinguish themselves in rowing at Harvard and Princeton, but in a tragic parallel to what would befall one of his Kent crews two decades later, the fourth member was killed "in a pretty bad accident" before ever making it to college.

Perry's athletic career at Dartmouth got off to an igno-minious start when he was put on academic probation after the first semester, prohibiting him from participating in sports until his grades improved. He was able to row again his sophomore year, alternating between junior varsity and varsity lightweight boats. By his junior year in 1953, however, he had been "growing the wrong way" and had become too heavy for lightweight rowing and too short for heavyweights. Wanting to stay connected to the sport, he ended up coaching the freshman lightweight crew to a fairly successful year. The next fifty years would see his unbroken commitment to the sport of rowing as coach, race official, regatta steward, and recipient of dozens of awards and honors, including induction into four athletic halls of fame. Ultimately, five racing shells and five trophies would be named in his honor. By the turn of the twenty-first century, the young man who had to give up competing in the sport because of his size had become its most visible advocate.

———

Nineteen fifty-three was also the last truly productive year for writer Mary Roberts Rinehart, whose short story "The Frightened Wife" had fetched $30,000 from the *Saturday Evening Post* and had also anchored a short story collection of the same name that was to be her last original book. Otherwise, the world seemed to be passing her by.

She had, after all, been born in the year of the nation's centennial, 1876, when, in the words of one biographer,

"Civil War veterans were still young men." Her family had become impoverished by the Panic of '93, a depression so swift and severe that many took their own lives, including her father. She lied about her age to go to nursing school, and later work, at Pittsburgh's Homeopathic Hospital, a gritty, disturbing experience that exposed her to, as she described it, "life in the raw": mutilated prostitutes, amputations without anesthetic, abandoned children dying from typhoid fever, and injured laborers "brought in and forgotten." The one blessing from her experience was that she had met a young doctor, Stanley Marshall Rinehart, who was especially popular in the children's ward. "He loved children," she later recalled. "He would walk in, apparently very severe, looking through his pince-nez at the children, and they would rush to him and surround him. He was very gentle with them, and he would play with them."

Mary Roberts married Stan Rinehart in April 1896, and a year later their first son, Stanley Jr., was born, followed by another son in 1900 and yet another in 1902. By this time she had fallen into the more traditional role of housewife, though she was responsible for sending out Dr. Rinehart's bills and providing assistance wherever she could as a trained nurse. Still, she found her life terribly confining: She recalled a ten-year stretch where she had never been out to dinner, and seven years straight of sleeping in the same bed. Her escape was to find time while the boys were at school and Dr. Rinehart was making his rounds to write short stories and poems, some of which magazines such as *Munsey's* had started to pay her for. In 1904 Stan and Mary were at last able to get away to New York for a bit of a respite, but in the most miserable of coincidences, during a visit to the New York Stock Exchange they witnessed firsthand a panic that wiped out their savings. Now over $12,000 in debt, she was "forced to write." At that moment, what started out as a hobby became a profession.

Fortunately, success, followed by fame, came quickly. After selling dozens of short stories, poems, essays, plays, and film scripts over the next five years, she finally broke out with a best-selling mystery novel, *The Man in the Lower Ten*, in 1909. Over the following twenty-seven years she wrote nine more top-ten best-selling novels in addition to several nonfiction collections, a popular autobiography, and literally hundreds of stories and articles for the leading magazines of the day, particularly *Ladies' Home Journal* and the *Saturday Evening Post*. As a journalist she became the first American correspondent at the Belgian front at the outbreak of World War I and in 1916 covered the national political conventions for the Philadelphia *Public Ledger* syndicate. Important for the purposes of this story because it made my arrival possible some thirty-six years later, at a quiet dinner at the Ritz sometime during 1917, Rinehart's eldest son, Stan—handsomely decked out in the uniform of his regiment and soon bound for France—was introduced to Mary Doran, daughter of publisher George Henry Doran. Their subsequent courtship evidently survived the adversities of time and distance, and they married in May 1919.

But the union of the two families had already been locked up in a different way two months before, when Stanley Marshall Rinehart Jr. became an employee of the George H. Doran Company, his employment partially secured by a gift of $25,000 in the company's capital stock from his mother. In 1927 Doran attempted to sell his business to Stan Rinehart and his brothers and ease into retirement but was strangely rebuffed. Doran instead chose to merge with Doubleday, Page & Company, a move he later came to deeply regret. After the merger the Rinehart men became directors of Doubleday, Doran & Company, but as Doran later recalled, "We [Doran and Frank N. Doubleday] failed to reckon that inevitably Doubleday children and Doran children might come into conflict with Doubleday Doran children. Rather quickly the effects of our parental blunders became manifest." On the eve of the Great Depression, Stan Rinehart and his brothers, largely backed by Mary Roberts Rinehart, struck out on their own with the publishing enterprise known as Farrar & Rinehart, a firm that would, in the words of one observer, compile "one of the most astonishing records any house ever turned in during a period of hard times."

Mary Roberts Rinehart's last "serious" novel—that is, one that wasn't a mystery or a romance, the genres she was known for—was *A Light in the Window,* a 1948 saga of an American book-publishing family from the World War I armistice to the dawn of the nuclear age. The book concludes with the third generation about to take over the family firm, a plea for tradition and continuity in a tumultuous time if ever there was one. Perhaps she had in the back of her mind her enigmatic grandson George and his singular lack of ambition to follow his father, Stan, in the publishing business, though for a time he tried his hand at selling college textbooks on the road and editing a few technical volumes. Indeed, George seemed more obsessed with music, martinis, and a kind of genteel mayhem than he did business, and in a move that stunned his parents because of his many talents, both intellectual and practical, he had even dropped out of Harvard at the end of his junior year. His only clear ambition, if it could be called that, was to marry his fiancée, Sharon Bonner, just as soon as she finished high school.

My mother's genealogical path to marriage with my father had a more traditionally American look. While a backward glance at Dad's roots had the Robertses and the Rineharts disappearing into a kind of early-nineteenth-century tangled obscurity, scrupulous records from my mother's family proved her to be directly descended from one of the first citizens of New Amsterdam and for a time the province's acting secretary, Hendrik Hendricksen Kip. (A descendant of Kip's—we're not quite sure which one—farmed the part of Manhattan between present-day Twenty-fourth and Thirty-third Streets along the East River, at a time when the river formed a bay there. Though the bay is now filled in, the neighborhood is still known as Kips Bay.) Perhaps intimidated by the British takeover of the province in 1664 and subsequent change of name to New York, Kip's grandson Jacob moved up the Hudson River around the turn of the eighteenth century to found a village that no longer exists, Kipsburg. A century and a half later, a descendant, Eliza Kittle Pitcher, would marry a prominent farmer, James Robert Kerley, himself descended from French Huguenots who had anglicized their name from deKerlé to fully assimilate into American society. Today, residents of Red Hook, New York, still refer to an outlying part of their town as Kerley Corners.

The first prominent Kerley to break with the family farming tradition was my great-grandfather, Charles Gilmore Kerley, who may have been the Dr. Benjamin Spock[*] of his generation. The vanguard of a return of the family to Manhattan, he settled there after medical school and quickly rose to prominence in the field of pediatrics, particularly specializing in the diseases of children. A consulting pediatrist, as they called it then, to several area hospitals, he was president of the American Pediatric Society from 1907 to 1908 and author of a widely used textbook, *The Practice of Pediatrics.* His fame and presumably modest fortune enabled him to buy a brownstone at 10 East Eighty-first Street, where he and his wife raised two daughters, Barbra and Priscilla. (10 East, as it came to be known, stayed in the family for seventy years and was always our home away from home after my family moved to Connecticut.)

---

[*] Those who know Spock's biography also know that in addition to his prominence as a pediatrician, he was a superb amateur oarsman, winning a gold medal at the 1924 Olympics.

My grandmother, Priscilla Kerley, was a mischievous, daring girl whose bohemian lifestyle was a clear rejection of her parents' Victorian values. She wed a man by the name of Myles Tierney while in her teens and quickly (and suspiciously) bore a son by him in 1925. Very soon thereafter she left Tierney for a writer she had fallen in love with, Charles William Bonner Jr. They had two children, a son in 1928, followed by my mother in 1931. Fortunately for the young family, Charles Bonner was hitting his writing stride in the teeth of the Depression, and after selling film rights to one of his novels, *Legacy,* he moved the family to Los Angeles to work on that and other scripts. (The book and the film—retitled *Adam Had Four Sons*—were based loosely on my grandfather's childhood in Brooklyn and starred Ingrid Bergman, Susan Hayward, Fay Wray, and June Lockhart, among others. An online reviewer recently wrote that the film reminded him "of a nervous speaker who spends too much time on the introduction and then suddenly realizes there's no time left for the story and conclusion.")

World War II brought change of the unwelcome kind to both America and the Bonners. Alcohol abuse, that great crucible of relationships, prompted my grandparents to divorce, though they put out the story—perhaps in an attempt to protect the children—that they still loved each other. (Alcohol also doomed Charles Bonner's brief career in the O.S.S. Family lore has it that he was sent to South Africa on a mission to rendezvous with another agent. He got drunk the night before the meeting, however, and forgot the secret phrase that would have gained him access to the man.) Priscilla's mother and father died in 1942 and 1945, respectively, and upon her father's death she moved the family into 10 East. By her fortieth birthday in 1947 she was in love again, this time with a recent immigrant from the Netherlands who had distinguished himself fighting the Nazis in the Dutch Underground. They married in April of that year, enabling her to take on a name that came to sound like something out of fairy-tale royalty: Priscilla van der Laan. (Or, as some used to say behind her back, Priscilla V.D.)

My parents were married on June 16, 1950, with all the usual suspects (and then some) assembled at the reception at 10 East. Photographs show an elderly Mary Roberts Rinehart looking a little out of place, like an aging quarterback who had just been pulled from the lineup and replaced with a young upstart. For one day, at least, the great matriarch had to yield to her grandson.

After my father impregnated my mother in early 1953, there was whispered hope that it would be a boy, if only to reinforce the tradition of primogeniture, which in a generation would come to be viewed as an atavistic, even sexist notion in the civilized world. So, when I finally made my appearance on September 30, 1953, Mary Roberts Rinehart was said to be very pleased. As disappointed as she may have been in her grandson, here was hope that the family would be reenergized, and maybe even accomplish something extraordinary again, as she had hinted through her characters in *A Light in the Window.* But the extraordinary, like true love, often comes to those who neither expect it nor feel they deserve it, as the oldest member of the Kent School, Class of 1972, would find out some eighteen and a half years later.

II
PATER'S DREAM

No school reflects the personality and characteris-
tics of its founder better than Kent School reflects
Father Sill's. In its devotion to religion, to self-
dependence, to the highest ideals of scholarship, it
bears his mark indelibly. Even its prowess in crew
racing stems directly from Father Sill . . .
—*New York Herald Tribune,* July 21, 1952

It's simply counterintuitive to think that the inspiration
for creating an elite boys' boarding school in northwestern Connecticut would come from anyone other than a
New England Brahmin concerned with self-perpetuation,
but in many ways Kent School was—for at least its first
fifty years or so—answering to a different sort of calling.
For one thing, it was founded by a thirty-two-year-old
Episcopal monk from New York City, Father Frederick
Herbert Sill, who in March 1906 had been granted permission from the Order of the Holy Cross, the Benedictine
Anglican monastery to which he belonged, to establish a
school. As Sill wrote in a modest prospectus, the school
would "provide at a minimum cost for boys of ability
and character, who must presumably upon graduation be
self-supporting, a combined academic and commercial

course of instruction, and also preparation for college and university courses. Simplicity of life, self-reliance, and directness of purpose are to be especially encouraged in the boys."

"Adopting a revolutionary premise of sliding scale tuitions," one commentator explained, "Father Sill changed boarding-school education from a refuge for the children of the wealthy to a training ground for future leaders in a democratic society." Sill's approach to the school was no doubt informed by his larger-than-life father, Rev. Thomas H. Sill, who after the Civil War established a Mission for Trinity Church in the Tenderloin district of New York City. For forty-five years Thomas Sill not only operated the mission chapel but also served as chaplain of the children's hospital and warden for a home for crippled children. His effect on the community was no better conveyed than in this observation from an eyewitness at Sill's funeral in 1910:

Frederick Herbert Sill, Order of the Holy Cross. *Courtesy of Kent School*

The night before the funeral, as the body lay in St. Chrysostom's Chapel and mourners came to take a farewell look at the face of him they loved so well, it was a study to note the classes represented. Now a man of wealth and standing in his community, following him a poor woman, then a stalwart policeman in his uniform, after him a letter carrier, then one of the young men of the choir, and so it went on, through the night.

Serendipity placed Frederick Herbert Sill's new school near the small town of Kent, which in 1906 was perhaps best known as a stop for the New York, New Haven, and Hartford Railroad as it wound its way to and from Montreal. Asked to bring communion to one of the town's residents, while visiting Kent he was taken on a ride along the west bank of the Housatonic River, behind which rose the region's highest feature, Mount Algo, and beyond which Macedonia Creek gave life to farm fields and pastures. Most important for a former Columbia University coxswain and rowing enthusiast, though, Sill was no doubt taken by the fact that here was a section of the Housatonic that was wide, smooth, and deep for perhaps two miles. Framed by rapids to the north and a dam on the south, this part of the river was even blessed with two long reaches—plenty of room for a crew to get in a 500-meter set of power strokes before having to round a bend. Described by one historian as not only a "visionary" and a "man of faith" but also "the consummate businessman," that same day Sill placed down a rental deposit of $10 on a run-down farmhouse above the banks of the Housatonic.

The Kent School debuted rather inauspiciously on September 28, 1906. Though some work (such as the installation of a bathroom) had been done on the farmhouse the preceding summer, beds hadn't arrived by opening day, and Sill had wildly and amusingly misjudged the dietary needs of the school's first twenty students and three masters. "I think that I ordered enough Shredded Wheat for the whole school for the entire year," he recalled on the school's thirtieth anniversary. "The canned baked beans lasted two years." The boys' first meal was a disaster but inadvertently gave rise to Kent's famous "self-help" philosophy. A family of four had been hired to cook and serve meals, but since the father was something of a malcontent and the daughter suffered from tuberculosis, it fell to mother and son to do the job. But the mother got sick halfway through cooking a batch of corncakes, and when the son went to serve them (Sill had baked them himself) he slipped on the freshly waxed dining room floor, pulled himself up, and walked out, never to return. The boys then simply waited on themselves and their guests, starting a tradition at Kent that lasted nearly three-quarters of a century.

As *Time* magazine reported twenty-one years after the school's debut, Sill's conversation with the boys following the dining-room debacle went something like this: "You fellows can make beds?" "Yes." "You can sweep floors?"

Father Sill and his first Kent class in 1906. *Courtesy of Kent School*

"Absolutely." "Well," Sill concluded satisfactorily, "I can cook eggs." *Time* explained:

> *The beds-floors-eggs incident was the beginning of a student-supervised, student broom-wielding system, which runs the school to this day. Students regulate discipline, keep order in study hall, wait on tables, manage the athletic teams, keep the equipment—from footballs to library books—in order. Wealthy boys and boys of moderate means are treated alike. The system is based solely on individual merits, with upperclassmen at the helm.*

With a dilapidated farmhouse as its anchor, Sill worked indefatigably and quickly—and with virtually no money—

to expand the school. In spring 1907 he found a farmstead upriver with enough buildings to service what he optimistically presumed to be the school's soon-to-be-swelling ranks. His offer to the farm's owners—$3,000 cash and a $3,000 mortgage—was secured with an earnest payment of $50 (which he had to borrow). Given three weeks to raise the cash, he hopped the first train for New York City and began a period of what he referred to as tough work. But he managed to raise the money by the requisite deadline and present a check for $3,000 to the owner of the farm, Miss Lizzie Fuller, securing a deed to the property. "Because [Fuller] belonged to the small group who believed the school would fail," however, the title to the property and mortgage papers would be withheld until the loan was paid in full.

Because of Sill's relentless energy and "directness of purpose," Kent School began to build a sense of legitimacy with the audacious purchase of the Fuller farm. After the school incorporated as Kent School Corporation, Sill immediately set about raising $25,000, telling prospective donors that the funds would go to "furnishing, heating, etc., as well as actual construction. The proposed buildings will provide for 32 boys and five masters, beside those engaged in household work."

True to his plan, Sill enrolled thirty-two students in fall 1907, and his fund-raising efforts were presumably successful, as renovation and construction were ongoing over the next several years. Two years later construction on a "main" wooden building was completed; in 1911 came a barn and infirmary; and in 1913 the centerpiece to the campus, St. Josephs Chapel, rose above the Housatonic. Impressively, ten years after it had been founded, Kent School boasted an enrollment of 131 boys taught by ten masters. (Sill saved money by teaching Sacred Studies, Latin, Greek, and English himself; he also for a time coached the football, hockey, and tennis teams.)

It was soon alarmingly apparent, however, that if the school was to survive it would not do so in wooden clapboard structures. In November 1911 a fire broke out in the mathematics classroom in the main building, but thanks to the quick response of the farm's superintendent as well as the "well-trained school fire brigade," the flames were quickly doused. The fire only fueled Sill's desire to establish a "permanent" Kent, one in which fireproof brick buildings would come to symbolize his commitment to future generations of Kent students. Once again, Sill's remarkable tenacity pulled it off, and throughout the 1920s and 1930s the campus began to take on a Georgian air as handsome redbrick buildings started to replace the wooden firetraps.

The one exception to the general architectural uniformity of the Kent campus would be the new chapel. Befitting Sill's monastic way of life, a Norman design was chosen, one that reflected "the heritage of ecclesiastical architecture in England and France during the eleventh and twelfth centuries, the period when the great monastic movement of St. Bernard and so many others were in their heyday."

Made of local field stone (some from old stone walls) and built on a rise slightly above the rest of the campus, its tall, impressive bell tower would be visible for miles up and down the Housatonic, calling attention to Sill's extraordinary vision—and faith. The bell tower itself would contain ten 1,500-hundred-pound bells cast at the Whitechapel Bell Foundry in London, permitting what is known as change-ringing, or the art of ringing individual bells according to a nonmelodic, mathematical pattern. Work began on the new St. Joseph's Chapel in June 1930, and it was officially consecrated the following year.

Sill's growing reputation as an educator and a visionary was such that by the 1920s the waiting list to get into Kent was growing unmanageably long. Sill partially addressed this problem by buying another farmhouse five miles away at South Kent and installing two of his prefects from the class of 1918 as masters. The school would be known (not so cleverly) as South Kent and as "not a twin, but an independent 'younger brother'" of Kent. (The Kent Idea, as it came to be known, had two other offspring, both founded by Kent alums: Midland School in California started in 1932 by Paul Squibb, class of 1914, and St. Luke's School in Texas, which was opened in 1941 by Walter W. Littell, '28. Both schools adopted Kent's self-help program as well as the notion of sliding-scale tuition.)

Since Father Sill's influence was still deeply felt when we rowed the sleek new racing shell named for him in 1972, it's worth recalling the reflections of others about this truly remarkable man. In an article for *Reader's Digest* in 1961 titled "The Most Unforgettable Character I've Met," Anson Gardner, one of the first twenty students to arrive at Kent that memorable September afternoon in 1906, amusingly recalled the first impression Sill made on him.

> *. . . short and slight, with a frank boyish face and stringy, straw-colored hair plastered so flat against his forehead that it looked almost painted on. His monastic habit resembled a billowing white nightgown topped with a broad shoulder cowl that flapped like a hen's wings when he flailed his arms to emphasize a point . . . So radiant was the enthusiasm of this odd white apparition, often referred to later as the Great White Tent, that we assembled that night and gave him the first of thousands of Kent cheers to ring up and down the lovely Housatonic Valley.*

"By all the laws of logic and economics," Gardner noted, "the school should not have survived." Four months prior to opening the school, Sill had sent out a prospectus to 1,500 wealthy and well-connected people in an effort to raise $250,000 for the school, but he "received exactly six answers and $300." His response was typically sanguine: "Well, if the Lord wants me to make a school with $300, I will do it." (One of the six responses came from Princeton president Woodrow Wilson, who liked "very thoroughly"

Sill's vision for the school. Responding to another Sill missive in 1907, Wilson unreassuringly promised to "watch the development of the school with the greatest sympathy.")

"Once Pater, as we later came to call him, committed himself to a job," Gardner recalled, "he hung on like a bulldog." Gardner gave as example the morning the boys awakened to a frozen main water pipe. Since the boys couldn't wash, they naturally thought they could sleep in a bit. Not so with Father Sill: He immediately formed a bucket brigade out to a nearby well. "If the water would not come to us, then we would go to the water." That same winter the school lost its ability to buy coal on credit, but "by this time, financial dilemmas were as familiar to us as algebra, and we eagerly awaited the solution." Sill and the boys simply went into the woods with saws and axes and cut firewood until the budget was again in balance, and even managed to make a profit selling logs to be used as railroad ties.

Whether it was an outgrowth of these experiences or the school's "simplicity of life" philosophy, frugality was the watchword even as the school established a stable financial footing. When enrollment grew to the point that it became necessary to hire a business manager, Sill even had him count matches to determine which brand offered the most per box, believing the school could save a little money. "By golly, he's right," the accountant begrudgingly admitted. Indeed, Sill's only indulgence was a yellow Stutz Bearcat, a luxury for which he could be forgiven, as the car was frequently used to ferry priests across the Hudson to the Order of the Holy Cross monastery and back. Boys who had some driving experience were often recruited as chauffeurs, a welcome perk whenever Sill was invited to tea at Miss Porter's School for Girls in Farmington. (And such a perquisite was not to be scoffed at: As one journalist commented, during Sill's reign, girls crossed the bridge from the town of Kent to the school "with approximately the same frequency as Martians." A dance wasn't permitted at the school until 1940, and at one dance musicians failed to show, "so Father Sill himself played the fiddle—interrupting himself periodically to give overexuberant couples a smart rap with his bow.")

But Gardner also recalled that Sill spared no expense when it came to helping Kent graduates who might "hit snags in college." "Telephone me, *collect*," he would often insist, even though those calls would ultimately cost him thousands of dollars. Father Sill's devotion to his boys was no better illustrated than in an anecdote that Gardner recounts from Thanksgiving Day 1938. Since students in those days remained on campus for the holiday, Sill made it a point to make it a memorable day for them, especially for the younger boys for whom it might have been the first Thanksgiving away from home. After a celebratory communion and dinner and some general mingling with the boys, Gardner wrote, "He quietly left for his family's home, without revealing what he had known since early dawn: that his mother had died suddenly during the night."

So what sort of boys was Sill turning out? If modest literary celebrity is any measure, then the answer is some pretty interesting ones. Among Kent's earliest graduates were three future Pulitzer Prize winners: musician Roger Sessions (class of 1911), poet Robert S. Hillyer (1913), and novelist James Gould Cozzens (1922). Sessions actually won the Pulitzer twice, first in 1974 as a special prize for his life's work and again in 1982 for his final work, "Concerto for Orchestra." Hillyer, who won his Pulitzer in 1934 for his *Collected Verse*, recalled that Father Sill "had the insight and wisdom to let an imaginative boy like me follow his own devices apart from athletics and groups—a dispensation for which I express gratitude to this day." Although Cozzens is probably best known for the novel *By Love Possessed*, he won his Pulitzer in 1949 for the World War II novel *Guard of Honor*. Befitting a man known to be brusque at times—he once told a *Time* reporter that "I can't read ten pages of Steinbeck without throwing up"—Cozzens's recollection of Kent was a bit more prosaic than Hillyer's. "Kent," Cozzens said, "marked me for life. If there is hard work to be done and I get out of it, I feel extremely guilty." Cozzens had even published an article on Kent's unique self-help philosophy for the *Atlantic Monthly* while still a student there.

Cozzens's *Guard of Honor* was based loosely on his World War II experience in the United States Army Air Force Office of Information Services, where he "became arguably the best informed officer of any rank and service in the nation." As

Kent World War II veterans go, though, Cozzens was one of the lucky ones. Forty-two Kent graduates were killed during the war, and the school itself had to make changes in 1942 to accommodate revisions to the Selective Service Act that called for the near-mandatory drafting of all eighteen-year-old boys with few exemptions for college. In order to make certain that boys earned enough credits to graduate before they turned eighteen, changes were made in the curriculum to fast-track the older students and the school stayed open year-round, adding a summer session.

Unfortunately, during this critical period for the school and the nation, Father Sill could only offer symbolic, if still omnipresent, leadership. At the age of sixty-six in 1940 he suffered what Anson Gardner called "the first in a series of paralyzing strokes that forced him from the headmaster's chair to a wheelchair." On March 1, 1941, he submitted his resignation to the Father Superior of the Order of the Holy Cross, which was still largely responsible for the school. Writing that he was very happy with his decision, Sill asked that "all friends of Kent School . . . consider this as expressing my own personal approval of this step . . . and I will look forward with pleasure to serving the school to the best of my ability." Sill's announcement moved Hillyer to scratch out a sonnet, the last few lines of which no doubt captured the sentiments of many.

> *Then, as Mount Algo gathers in the sun,*
> *We go with you, and as the light grows dim,*

The Chapel dawns with candles, one by one;
The Eternal Day sounds through the evening hymn.
God rest you merry, Pater. God's content.
Bless you as you have blessed the men of Kent.

Pater's successor was Father William Scott Chalmers, of necessity also a member of the Order of the Holy Cross, but a priest who had already served Kent School for two years prior to his formal appointment as headmaster. Chalmers immediately faced the daunting task of not only operating a school during wartime but also of succeeding the enigmatic Father Sill. "Imagine trying to step into the shoes of a legend," writes Joan Beattie in her history of the school, "while that legend was alive and living at the school." According to another observer, "With the passing of the torch from Pater, the founder, to a successor-administrator, the financial footing of the school was soft and tremulous at best. This situation did not improve in the time that Fr. Chalmers was there . . . the reason might well have laid in the nature of people [investors] who wait to see if an institution can survive the passing power of the founder."

Still, as the 1941 school year began, Kent boasted thirty-five faculty and 308 students paying an average tuition of $900—"very much in line with Father Sill's estimate that tuition should equal the cost of a mid-size car," according to Beattie. Because upperclassmen were being drafted into the armed services as they turned eighteen, Chalmers had to admit a disproportionately larger number of younger students to keep enrollment level from year to year, a task at which he seems to have succeeded. When workers at the school's dairy farm left to take far more lucrative jobs in manufacturing in Hartford or Bridgeport as part of the war effort, Chalmers put out a call for volunteers to take their place; fully a third of the student body signed up, some of the boys no doubt thinking such work would help them foil the government-imposed rationing of dairy products like ice cream. (They were right.) Finally, Chalmers was able to complete the last building in Father Sill's plan for the "Permanent Kent" and even managed to retire some debt.

The biggest challenge of Chalmers's tenure, though, was the gradual secularization of the school's governance, beginning in 1943 when the first layman was elected to the Kent School board of trustees, hitherto composed exclusively of members of the Order of the Holy Cross. In 1945 the Order disengaged all but spiritually from the operation of the school, possibly thinking that in the competitive postwar environment the school needed competent businessmen and not monks to guide it into the uncertain future. Because he wanted to remain headmaster at Kent, Chalmers resigned from the Order of the Holy Cross and transferred to the Oratory of the Good Shepherd, another monastic community of Anglicans in Wappingers Falls, New York, "dedicated as deeply to poverty, chastity, and obedience." He stayed on at Kent for four more years, concluding in his letter of resignation in March 1949 that during his tenure, Kent had "moved from the small school of the earlier years to the established institution of the present and future." All this under the watchful (and no doubt critical) eye of Father Sill, wheelchair-bound and practically without speech, but still a force to be reckoned with.

While recollections of Chalmers are few, we know from one anecdote that he had a pretty good sense of humor. When John Elliott—father of Fred Elliott, our number-three man on the 1972 crew—stood before his first job assembly as senior prefect, he was stricken with stage fright. "I stood up, stuttered, got nervous, and finally said softly, 'Oh, shit,' and sat down," he recalled. Another prefect read the days' announcements instead. Following the assembly Father Chalmers came over to Elliott, patted him on the shoulder, and said, "Great speech."

Chalmers's successor was Rev. John Oliver Patterson, who was not only responsible for the remade Kent as I found it when I first arrived on the campus in September 1968 but also for broader changes in the way the Episcopal Church operated. Along with three other priests he founded the Associated Parishes for Liturgy and Mission in 1946, using their own parishes to experiment with changes both ceremonial and social. As Joan Beattie explains:

Much of what we take for granted today in the Episcopal Church is the result of their vision: the Eucharist as the main service on Sundays, the offertory procession in which the bread and wine are brought to the altar, the gospel procession that brings the

*reading of the gospel into the congregation, and
"music that all could sing."*

Patterson and his colleagues also sought to link the
church favorably to emerging social issues such as racial
justice, a move toward tolerance and liberalism that would
ironically split the church (over the ordination of gays)
some fifty years later. Since education was a significant
part of this movement, Kent no doubt proved to be a tempt-
ing laboratory for an energetic priest with a background in
architecture who was "obsessed with concepts" that could
be "worked into brick and mortar."

Patterson differed from his predecessors in other ways
as well. Significantly, he was not a member of any order
but rather a husband, father, and parish priest from Madi-
son, Wisconsin. If Father Sill's continued presence at Kent
was intimidating to him, he never betrayed the notion but
rather described his mission in simple, bold, language. "I
can state my goal for Kent quite briefly," he said upon arriving in the fall of 1949, "that it be without question the finest
possible Christian school. Our aim is not merely to turn out
educated men, but educated Christian men—men who can
find real stature in the universe." The first phase of Patterson's plans for Kent was to make drastic improvements
to the school's physical property, including a new gym,
boathouse, auditorium, library, and art gallery—all to be
completed by the school's fiftieth anniversary in 1956. The
plan also included construction of a new rectory designed

by Patterson himself, a design that would ultimately quote much from the work of Frank Lloyd Wright.

Patterson as well as the Kent community in general paused from its ambitious advance into the future when Father Sill passed away peacefully on July 17, 1952. On July 21 the *New York Herald Tribune* eulogized Sill not in the obituary section but on its editorial page:

> *Men who die leave various achievements behind them to stand as their memorials. The Rev. Dr. Frederick Herbert Sill . . . leaves behind him a truly living memorial—a school. . . . Today Kent's physical establishment is valued at $1,500,000 and it is invariably ranked as one of America's foremost boy's schools. Yet one feature of that first semester in 1906 continues unchanged to these days. Kent boys did their own chores then, and they do them now. For at Kent education includes an understanding of the eminently valuable art of sweeping the floor.*

The *Time* magazine issue of July 28 also trumpeted the Sill legacy, praising the Kent system where "sons of rich and poor still share alike in the chores, while their parents work out with the school just how much tuition they can afford to pay."

In an essay written for Kent's fiftieth anniversary titled "FHS: A Faith That Did Not Fail," James Gould Cozzens soberly suggested that "when Pater died . . . men of the early classes must have said to themselves: There's the end of Kent School. Grounds for that sad surmise were not hard

to find. . . . The difference, the change, had been not so much seen as felt." But by the end of the essay Cozzens had talked himself out of his gloom, positing that the school's future leaders would "grasp" and "cherish" Sill's faith and "with devotion like his own, gladly serve. They would serve as he had served—not in

Father Sill in the twilight of his life. *Courtesy of Kent School*

mechanical rehearsings of any past, but in creative renewing." And thus did Cozzens justify, however inadvertently, Kent's emergence from beneath the monastic robes of the Order of the Holy Cross and into the modern, and increasingly classically liberal, Christian idea of education.

This was no better demonstrated than in the school's association with other Christian leaders who were pushing for racial equality, particularly those who were seeking an end to apartheid in South Africa. Alan Paton, founder of the South African Liberal Party and author of the acclaimed antiapartheid novel *Cry, The Beloved Country,* lectured at Kent several times during the 1950s and helped found the school's honor society, known as the Guild. And on the occasion of Father Sill's birthday dinner on March 10, 1956—one of many events held in celebration of the school's fiftieth anniversary—the keynote speaker was Rev. Trevor Huddleston, a venerated antiapartheid activist and mentor to a young black fellow cleric by the name of Desmond Tutu. Huddleston told the gathering that South Africa's educational system "is not an educational system at all. It is a system of indoctrination aimed, and intentionally aimed, at the preserving of racial ideology. Nothing could be further from the Christian ideal."

Huddleston's bitter tone was no doubt informed by an incident from the previous year that unwittingly placed Kent in the midst of a shameful international scandal. Putting its money where its ideological mouth was, during the spring of 1955 Kent had offered a full scholarship to a black South African boy of Huddleston's choosing. Huddleston selected a student from his own parish, St. Peter's Anglican Mission in Johannesburg, who "was qualified in every way" to make the grade at Kent. The sixteen-year-old, Stephen Ramasodi, was "not only the brightest boy in his class," as *Time* magazine reported, "he is also a whiz in science and hopes someday to be a doctor." But after a thorough grilling by detectives "on every topic, from why he wanted to go to the U.S. to what he thought what was wrong with education at home," Ramasodi was ultimately refused a passport.

As one official of the government pathetically explained, "Frankly, [he] would be taught things he could never use when he came back to South Africa. Why should we let the boy be frustrated by being led to hope for things he can never have in this country?"

Under Father Patterson's leadership Kent was, indeed, "starting to reach out to the world at large" in "bold and daring" moves to diversify its student population. In 1957 the school's board of trustees asked Kent graduate and future secretary of state Cyrus Vance to form a committee to study, among other things, "the feasibility of establishing a girls' school of Christian intent." This was specifically tasked to a member of the class of 1931 who had been much admired by Father Sill, Sidney N. Towle. Towle presented his recommendations in March 1958, which, significantly, called not for a strictly coeducational Kent but for a parallel school that would nevertheless combine with the existing boys school in a unified curriculum under the leadership of a single headmaster. Towle further suggested that the Vance committee take a look at a farmstead that had just gone up for sale as a possible campus. As if to underscore the parallel relationship to the boys' school, the farm was located five miles away on a mountaintop, a daunting trek for all but the most determined adolescent boy seeking a clandestine romantic liaison.

The plan for the girls' school was approved by a unanimous vote of the Kent School board of trustees, and ground was broken in May 1959. Later in the year Sidney Towle was appointed associate headmaster and principal of the girls' division of Kent School. As *Time* magazine commented, "Kent's mission (to produce soundly educated Christian citizens) was expanded in a way that would have almost surely left Father Sill blinking." And in a comment that may have been prescient for its time but sounds utterly silly today, "hard-headed" Father Patterson told the magazine that "in today's world men have to work effectively with women. Women are people as much as men."

The first girls arrived at Kent in September 1960, and two years later Father Patterson, having accomplished more at the school since Father Sill's plan for the permanent Kent, resigned to start yet another school, St. Stephen's in Rome, Italy, based on the Kent idea of self-help. Towle was elevated to the position of headmaster and saw it through the turbulent 1960s and 1970s, a time during which, as Kent historian Joan Beattie explains it, "the almost worshipful attitude toward Kent seen in [the school's own student-run] newspaper was replaced by criticism." While widely admired by many in the educational community for its outstanding faculty and curricula, the isolated campuses and generally ascetic Kent way of life led even *Time* magazine to refer to the school as akin to a Tibetan lamastery. A prison analogy was often invoked in describing Kent, "Sing Sing on the Housatonic" being the most common appellation in my day.

There was no question that Kent, among the pantheon of elite New England boarding schools, probably limited the liberties of its students more than most of its peer institutions. Towle, aware that the presence of girls would present new challenges to the school's order—even though at the start, intermingling with the boys was limited to a few honors classes and social events on the odd weekend—effectively doubled down on discipline, not so much introducing new restrictions as firmly enforcing those that were already in place. When my sister came to Kent in 1966, it was not permitted for any student to cross the Housatonic to enter the town of Kent. Students had just been granted a Thanksgiving holiday, but weekend leaves off campus were only allowed under the most dire of circumstances, such as a death in the family. A dress code was strictly enforced, and teachers were always to be referred to as masters, which became cause for much humor when a bright young English teacher with the unfortunate last name of Baiter was hired in the late 1960s.

As headmaster, Towle had one foot firmly entrenched in the school's past, another in the school's worrisome present, with perhaps a toenail remaining for its future. While not a "man of the cloth," Sidney Towle was not so much a favored student of Father Sill's as a disciple. Their admiration for each other had few bounds, Sill describing the younger Towle as "one of the outstanding boys of the school in personality, in efficiency, in popularity, in loyalty, in religious life." Towle had even been offered a job at Kent following his graduation from Yale in 1935 but declined. A law degree from Yale, service in wartime, and practice at a law firm in Boston all distracted Towle from involvement with Kent until the early 1950s. Once fully engaged with the school, however, he was determined to not let it stray from Father Sill's original vision for it, a vision that reflected Pater's disappointment with the "luxurious" environments of other church-affiliated schools, where common rooms were "like the lounges of city clubs" and "dining halls and service were fashioned after the style of the landed gentry of England." Towle unquestionably agreed.

This attitude left Kent behind other elite boarding schools when it came to liberalizing decorum and generally loosening up rules on how students should spend their free time. Significantly, many schools started to move away from their Christian foundations by dropping mandatory chapel attendance. (In 1972 Kent still required students to attend four services a week.) Believing that Kent was starting to lose its edge—in the 1960s the school had one of the poorest endowments of any New England boarding school—one administrator suggested to Towle that it might be easier for the school to attract gifts if it started to present itself in a more secular way.* Towle adamantly refused to consider this, even though he was financially burning the candle at both ends: paying top dollar for a first-rate faculty and academic facilities while handicapping the school's

---

* Although Kent characterized itself as a Christian school, that didn't mean "Christian only." In its move toward diversity in the 1950s, it started to attract students of all denominations, so that by the time I enrolled at the school Catholics were permitted to attend Mass in the town of Kent and services were available for Jewish students on Friday nights.

ability to build endowments on a magnitude of an Andover or Exeter. In doing so he was not so much committing the school to a vow of poverty as one of austerity, toeing the line of his mentor's call for "simplicity of life."

Conditions at Kent in the 1960s could best be described as Spartan, at least on the older boys' campus where some of the furnishings had been in use for thirty years or more. Most dorm rooms were simple affairs with rudimentary bunk beds and desks (the joke was that they had been rejected by the Salvation Army); in winter students were greeted every morning with a cold cement floor. TVs were not permitted in dorm rooms (though stereos were, only to be played during a narrow window following classes and before dinner) or even in common areas. Contact with the outside world was limited to four pay phones, mostly dominated in the evenings after dinner by boys checking on their girlfriends at home or at the Kent girls' campus. But because three hundred boys spent thirty minutes or more each day cleaning classrooms, picking up trash, dusting, sweeping, raking, or wiping down tables in the dining hall, the campus always had a tidy, if austere, look to it.

There was one notable exception to the school's generally frugal ways, however: School officials and alumni alike lavished money on a rowing program that had by the 1960s "made an impact on scholastic and collegiate rowing vastly disproportionate" to the school's small size. Its distinction from the school's other sports programs—in fact, from the school itself at times—was no better symbolized than in an appellation that suggested that it was to be considered an institution unto itself, with its own unique conventions and privileges. For to have earned membership in the Kent School Boat Club (KSBC) meant not only being among an elite few to have met a daunting physical challenge, it also offered the opportunity to "touch the world from many angles," as my great-grandfather Doran liked to say. Importantly, especially in a day when international travel was considered a once-in-a-lifetime experience for most, it offered the chance to go to England to compete in the Henley Royal Regatta.

III

WATER MUSIC

"There is nothing—absolutely nothing—half so much worth doing as simply messing about in boats."

—KENNETH GRAHAME, *THE WIND IN THE WILLOWS*

I have deliberately chosen not to interweave the history of Kent School with that of its premier sport to avoid leaving the impression that is unfortunately made on many—that Kent is that "rowing school." Though Father Sill could truly be described as a fanatic about the sport, his founding principles of simplicity of life, directness of purpose, and self-reliance didn't have as its corollary a really great crew. When I think about how an institution can get a reputation for something that is not part of its primary mission (like education), I am reminded of how a colleague once described the trade association to which I have belonged for over thirty years, Publishers Association of the West: "We are," he proclaimed, beer in hand, "a drinking association with a publishing problem."

In fact, Sill was careful not to introduce rowing until the school was on a sound financial footing. Rowing is an expensive sport. Though more sophisticated than the thin-skinned, wood boats of Sill's time, an elite carbon-fiber/

honeycomb/epoxy eight-man racing shell in 2009 could run over $30,000, not counting the oars, which can cost $300 each. Sill paid $800 for Kent's premier eight after rowing was finally introduced at the school in 1922, in today's dollars the equivalent of about $10,000. And the costs don't end there. Maintenance is ongoing for any competitive racing shell, but wood boats pose a unique problem, which partially explains why they're seldom rowed anymore: They are extremely fragile. Oarsmen get into a boat by first stepping onto a narrow, latticelike platform upon which also rests a seat and the runners for its slide. Since a wood boat's actual hull is only about one-eighth of an inch thick—thus the common reference to boats as shells—a misplaced foot can mean disaster. Other hazards include snags, submerged logs, and collisions with other boats. Wooden racing shells can certainly be repaired, but often the patch or repair can compromise a boat's performance, thus hastening obsolescence.

Interestingly, the transition from wood boats to their carbon-fiber descendants was probably the only significant technological innovation in the sport of rowing of the twentieth century. By the late nineteenth century most of the basic design and engineering that make for a fast racing shell had been worked out. But like all such evolutionary processes there was a lot of trial and error, odd technical digressions, and overnight revolutionary advances on the way toward transforming a vehicle initially meant for transportation, commerce, and harvesting waters into one exclusively intended for sport.

———

That humans have a fascination with speed is not so much a matter of satisfying a craving for an adrenaline fix as it is a derivative of our primal instinct that getting someplace first can improve not only the odds of success but survival itself as well. Translated into commerce, this meant that a herald on a fast horse had a better chance of keeping his job than a rival on a less competitive mount. So, too, with the watermen on the Thames in London in the seventeenth and eighteenth centuries, where goods and people were constantly being transported across, up, down, and around the river. (Because tens of thousands were employed on these liveries, Parliament closely regulated the industry and insisted that watermen spend several years in apprenticeships.) Speed obviously was an advantage. As rowing historian Bill Miller explains:

> It was very early on when one waterman decided to challenge another waterman or when one passenger urged his waterman on to a speedy passage that boat speed became an asset. A waterman could enhance his income by receiving a gratuity from his pleased patron or gain publicity and a reputation for winning contests. Racing between watermen soon flourished.

In 1716 actor Thomas Doggett founded a race for first-year apprentice watermen known as the Coat and Badge, an event that is still held every August 1 on the tideway in London, making it one of the oldest sporting events in the world. The winner was awarded, as one would expect, a coat and a badge, as well as the privilege of manning the Royal Barge whenever the King decided to take to the water. A Coat and Badge winner may have been aboard the Royal Barge on July 17, 1717, when it floated the Thames alongside another barge containing a small orchestra performing George Frideric Handel's *Water Music* for the first time. (So much did King George I admire the work that he asked the worn-out musicians to replay the three-suite piece not once but twice.)

Naturally, informal boat racing wasn't limited to the Thames. Across the Atlantic in New York City, according to Miller, "the steps at the end of Whitehall Street [at the tip of lower Manhattan] became the Grand Central of the water transport era. Soon races were contracted with rather large purses." Appropriately, a crude, four-oared racing wherry became known as a Whitehall, and in a famous race in 1824 from the Battery to Hoboken point and back one such craft, *American Star,* defeated the British Navy's *Certain Death.* The event, whose winners received the substantial sum of $1,000, was witnessed by 50,000 spectators.

Rowing officially became a collegiate sport in 1815 when Oxford formed several boat clubs for intramural competition. In 1818 two of London's boat clubs, the Star and the Arrow, merged to form the Leander Club, which later moved to Henley-on-Thames and to this day remains the oldest, largest, and most successful rowing club in the world, having won more Olympic and world championship gold medals than any other club. Cambridge introduced rowing in 1827, and two years later it was to challenge Oxford in eight-oared "cutters" to initiate one of the longest-running collegiate rivalries in the history of sport. (Oxford won the race before some 20,000 spectators.) The venue for the race was an unusual "reach" in the Thames at Henley, a gun-barrel-straight section of river nearly a mile and a quarter in length. Schoolboy rowing debuted the same year with a race between Eton and Westminster School in London.

No boat club (English or American) had yet taken advantage of a radical change in the hardware of rowing first introduced by Anthony Brown at Newcastle-on-Tyne in 1828, perhaps because it took over a decade to refine. There is no indication that outriggers (today known simply as riggers) were in use when the first Henley Regatta made its debut in 1839 either. But once Harry Clasper, also of Newcastle, perfected the iron rigger sometime in the early 1840s, it became possible to build narrower, faster boats, as the pivot point for the oar was removed from a boat's gunwale to an oarlock several feet out over the water. From this point forward, a racing shell needn't be much wider than an oarsman's posterior. The next logical development was to remove the keel of the boat and lay a thin "skin" over internal "bones" that would hold it all together. By 1856 an eight-oared boat embodying all these improvements, the *Victoria*, won the Grand Challenge Cup at the Henley Royal Regatta. And thus, according to Miller, "the age of the racing shell began."

But rowing was still primarily an exercise for an oarsman's upper body, and until someone could figure out
how to unharness the potential energy in his legs, rowing mechanics would still be far from efficient. This was
first addressed in the United States in the 1870s with the
development of the sliding seat, at first a modest affair with
perhaps half a foot of track. A decade later, though, longer
slides were in use so that an oarsman had a range of motion
that started with his knees nearly at his chest at the beginning of a stroke and finished with his legs flat as his oar
emerged from the water. As the author of *A Short History
of American Rowing,* Thomas Mendenhall, explains, "How
most effectively to combine back, legs, and arms would
henceforth become the central problem in the formulation
of any rowing style."

Along with the development of the sliding seat, the only
other significant advancements remaining were the addition of an adjustable "button" or "collar" on the oar where
it met the oarlock (to improve leverage) and redesigning
the oarlock itself so that it swiveled with each stroke. As
Bill Miller concludes, "In a matter of several years," rowing
was transformed "from an early nineteenth-century sport
to what we know as a modern twentieth-century application. . . . I can't think of any real significant changes in
shells and hardware all the way through until 1972."*

Though advancements in rowing technology were lib-
erally shared on both sides of the Atlantic, there was one

---

* When the first carbon-fiber boats were introduced to the Olympics
at the Munich games that year.

The evolution of the eight-oared racing shell. At left is the Oxford boat from 1929. By adding outriggers, eights were substantially slimmed down within one hundred years. *Author's Collection.*

significant social divide over how Great Britain and its former colony approached the sport: the definition of *amateur*. Rowing had become so popular in the United States by the mid- to late nineteenth century that it enjoyed a brief but scandalous era of the "professional oarsmen," or rowers who would compete for a cash prize. Professional rowing, however, was done in by its reputation for shady tricks, particularly collusion with gamblers. In 1872 the National Association of Amateur Oarsmen was formed, and over the next decade the definition of an amateur evolved into that of "a working man whose job or business would effectively prevent him from training as regularly or extensively as a professional," according to Thomas Mendenhall. The English idea of the amateur oarsman was significantly different, particularly excluding anyone who was "a mechanic, artisan, or laborer"—in other words, anyone who exercised his hands and arms regularly. As Mendenhall explains, this "reflected a social structure and tradition which held the amateur and gentleman to be synonymous." The conflicting views of what constituted an amateur were later to collide as Americans started to seek entry into English events such as the Henley Royal Regatta.

Rowing has the distinction of being the oldest intercollegiate sport in the United States, debuting in 1852 in a race between Harvard and Yale, decades before football and baseball started to gain traction and overwhelm rowing in popularity by both participants and spectators. It wasn't until well after the Civil War, though, that rowing became organized as a truly national sport, with crews from such schools as Wisconsin, Stanford, and California starting to compete in regional championships. In 1895 the newly formed Intercollegiate Rowing Association introduced a four-mile race for eights at Poughkeepsie, New York, to determine a national champion. The championship was won by Columbia University, whose coxswain was a diminutive twenty-one-year-old by the name of Frederick Herbert Sill. At a celebratory dinner following the races, according to Robert F. Kelley in his 1931 book *American Rowing: Its Background and Traditions*, "Hamilton Fish Jr. . . . No. 7 on the victorious Columbia crew, picked up the small coxswain . . . and threw him across the table" during a free-for-all brawl of unknown origin.

———

Father Sill introduced rowing to Kent on April 15, 1922, when a gig manned by two boys took to the Housatonic with Father Sill coaching from the coxswain's seat. The boys were not prepared for the river's swift current, however, and their efforts were further hampered by a poorly adjusted oarlock. The remains of a bridge in the middle of the river posed an immediate hazard, but Sill skillfully maneuvered the boat so that "a landing was effected . . . in such a way that little harm was done to the gig." Once the oarlock was readjusted, according to an article in the school's newspaper, the *Kent News*, the boat

> . . . started off downstream. . . . At a point about two miles down the river, the boat was turned around with its nose upstream, and the arduous task of making headway against a very swift current began.

Here the endurance of [the oarsmen] asserted itself,
and it was not long before the exponents of the first
crew in the history of Kent School rounded the bend
in the river and swung into shore under the new
boathouse.

The "new" boathouse was in fact a converted shed that already contained a small fleet of boats of various shapes and sizes: another gig, a centipede (a boat sculled by several oarsmen), and two eights. One would have to assume that the boats were not new, especially since they'd be taking some inadvertent abuse by rank newcomers to the sport, and competition worthy of the name was still a year off. At first Sill used only the two-man gigs to get the boys accustomed to the "swing" of competitive rowing; after a few weeks an eight took to the water. "For a short time . . . the rowing was rather awkward," Sill recalled, "but by the time the rowers got used to the shell they showed very good prospects. . . . Of course, we cannot expect to turn out a finished crew by June, but, through the start made this year, future crews will be developed with greater ease." Somewhat expectedly, in Kent's only extramural competition that year, the Yale Interscholastic Regatta, its first eight came in fifth.

Sill rewarded his own optimism for the future of Kent crew by ordering a brand-new, "first-class eight-oared shell" during the summer of 1922. As described by its builder, W. H. Davy & Sons of Cambridge, Massachusetts,

The first Kent crew in 1922. *Courtesy of Kent School*

the boat would be "sixty-one feet long, twenty-three inches beam, and nine-and-a-half inches deep, which is suitable for a 160-pound crew."* The first crew to use the boat in the spring of 1923 beat a Yale freshman boat and managed a second place in both the Yale and Harvard interscholastic regattas. Kent rowing rapidly climbed the ladder of success from there, turning out its first undefeated crew in 1926. The 1927 crew was equally as good, underscoring the success of a program that by now involved over a third of the school's 280 students. In addition to the elite first and

---

* If that seems light, it's important to remember that collegiate football linemen in 1922 seldom weighed over 200 pounds. As with football players, oarsmen have "grown" over time as advances in diet and training have enabled ever bigger athletes to literally pull their own weight. By way of example *Time* magazine referred to the 174-pound 1947 Kent crew as "brawny," while the 175-pound Kent crew twenty-five years later was often considered "lightweight."

second boats of the Kent School Boat Club, an intramural club system that put eight additional boats on the water each spring proved to be a sort of developmental league for nurturing future talent. The subject of a feature article in the *New York Times Magazine* on May 15, 1927, Kent's "youthful rowers" were said to "range in ability from the first-shell veterans to the eager amateurs of the tenth [boat], ludicrously varied in physical dimensions, but richly endowed with muscular energy."

Sometime during the winter of 1927 Sill quietly accepted an invitation to compete in the Henley Royal Regatta the following summer, an overture that was sweetened by the gift from newspaper magnate Lord Rothermere of a brand-new eight that would be waiting for the crew upon its arrival in England. (According to Christopher Dodd in his history of the regatta, "When standing on Henley bridge in the rain in the nonrowing season of 1921, [Sill] vowed he would send a Kent crew to the regatta within ten years.") As the *New York Times* reported, since "no American preparatory school has taken part in such a contest abroad" the announcement was "extensively heralded." The *Times* suggested that there was a "glamour about this conception of young American oarsmen, trained on an Indian river, crossing the sea to enter the lists on a waterway old enough to have memories of the blades of Roman galleys."

Sill was not happy about the publicity the announcement received, although one wonders what he might have been expecting. According to the *Times*, by 1927 the world

The first American schoolboy crew to compete at Henley was Kent in 1927.
Courtesy of Kent School

had already been "blazing an Emersonian trail to his door" because of the growing reputation of the Kent Idea. Still, Sill told the magazine that "too much publicity is one of the main difficulties connected with school sports. We do not enter the regatta as a championship crew or as representing anybody but ourselves." He continued, "We are going . . . for the profit to be derived from association with English rowing men. . . . I believe there are some features of English sportsmanship that it would be well for us in the United States to assimilate." As the *Times* concluded, in eschewing publicity "it is [Sill's] wish that simplicity of purpose be observed."

Father Sill's ascetic view of sportsmanship gave rise to a Kent School Boat Club ethos that was still very much in practice when I joined the club in 1972, for if there was a Kent Idea, there was also a Kent School Boat Club "idea."

That idea embodied the notion that, as representatives of the school and with occasional exposure on an international stage, KSBC oarsmen needed to be, quite frankly, rowing's equivalent of members of the Order of the Holy Cross. Humility was the watchword. Neither defeat nor victory was to be worn on one's sleeve. In competition "eyes were to stay in the boat," chitchat even among ourselves was frowned upon as one commits to a vow of silence in a monastery. This led to Kent crews' reputations of being if not snobbish then certainly enigmatic. Clean-cut and always uniformed in white until the 1990s, it was as if the vestigial shreds of the "great white tent" were a reach from the grave. But those who thought that KSBC's reticence was always genuine were naive. The argument that it was false modesty or that we were simply stuck up had some merit at times.

Because there was not yet a competition specifically for schoolboys at Henley in 1927, Kent had to compete for the Thames Challenge Cup, whose entrants ranged broadly from college freshman and lightweight crews, to English club crews, to American prep school crews. In its first (and only) heat, Kent had the misfortune to draw the ultimate winner of the trophy, the Thames Rowing Club, from a field of twenty-eight entrants. After trailing at the quarter-mile mark by a mere ten feet, the Thames crew pulled even with Kent by the half-mile mark, then overcame the Kent crew in the last hundred yards, winning by a quarter length. Still, it was the fastest heat of the event, and Thames faced no stiffer competition on their way to winning the cup. Kent returned to Henley in 1930 and fared a little better, actually making it to the final, where it again lost by the excruciatingly small difference of a quarter of a length.

Three years later, though, Kent rowing had arrived, as they say. The 1933 crew beat boats from Harvard, Yale, and a handful of schools, and had for the most part dominated them; only in the race with Harvard was the margin of victory less than a length. Kent had earned another trip to Henley, and even had a fan in the White House to wish them well. Offering "good wishes for a successful trip," President Franklin Roosevelt dashed off a brief note of encouragement to longtime acquaintance Father Sill before the crew sailed for England. Successful it was: Once again entered into the Thames Challenge Cup, Kent swept the

The 1933 Kent crew, winners of the Thames Challenge Cup. *Courtesy of Kent School*

THE WHITE HOUSE
WASHINGTON

May 24, 1933

My dear Father Sill:

I was interested to hear that you are taking another crew from Kent to the Henley Regatta this year and I am writing to offer my good wishes for a successful trip.   I am sure the presence of a crew of American school boys would be helpful in strengthening the ties between good sportsmen of the two countries and it all makes for better understanding.

Very sincerely yours,

Franklin D. Roosevelt

Rev. Frederick H. Sill, O.H.C.,
Kent School,
Kent, Connecticut.

Courtesy of Kent School

event, beating four English crews so soundly that the *London Times* rowing correspondent was moved to write, "The standard of rowing was not below average after all. Kent School were almost certainly the best crew that ever rowed in the Thames Cup."

Tote Walker. *Courtesy of Kent School*

In 1937 Father Sill stepped down as coach and was replaced by his assistant, T. Dixon "Tote" Walker, a member of the Kent class of 1919. With his rubberlike manner of expression and bushy eyebrows, he might have been mistaken for one of the Marx Brothers, but in fact his oarsmen recalled him as the apotheosis of the gentleman and a stickler for good sportsmanship. Walker would not let his crews win a race by more than two lengths, believing that "winning was enough." When one of his crews would seem to be pulling away by more than two lengths, "Get in your lane, Kent" was code language for the crew to ease off.*

Kent won the Thames Challenge Cup again in 1938 and 1947. The 1947 crew was undefeated on both sides of the Atlantic, winning all of its races by at least a length. Kent's growing reputation earned it a *Life* magazine cover story in the June 28, 1948 issue, its author declaring, "What football means to Notre Dame, rowing means to Kent." This was later underscored by a dominant 1950 crew that won all of its races, defeating Thames Rowing Club by two and a half lengths to once again capture the Thames Challenge Cup at Henley. (In previous heats it had beaten a Yale varsity lightweight crew by three lengths and a University College, Dublin, crew by two lengths.)

The triumphant 1950 crew also marked the end of something of an era for Kent rowing, an era that sought excellence in what had been quite frankly an elite sport husbanded by a handful of boarding schools and their nearby Ivy League kin. In the postwar years scholastic rowing expanded rapidly and even started to gain some traction in the public schools, particularly in the mid-Atlantic states. Colleges began enrolling ever more students with

---

* There was at least one notable exception. Prior to a race with Princeton, Walker had been verbally abused by the Tiger coach, who claimed that the rowing technique that Walker taught wasn't "correct" and that his boys would have to learn the sport all over again if they ever came to Princeton. As Kent moved two lengths up on Princeton during the race, no orders to ease up came from Walker. Kent won by seven lengths.

The 1950 Kent crew, undefeated on both sides of the Atlantic.
Courtesy of Kent School

considerable rowing experience, which led to bigger and stronger oarsmen and faster boats. The Thames Challenge Cup came to be dominated by American college crews, and since the embargo on international competition had yet to be lifted for the Princess Elizabeth Cup, Kent crews were on the outside looking in for a decade and a half as far as the Henley Royal Regatta was concerned. The sport was quite simply becoming more competitive at all levels.

Still, within the scholastic community, and even to a limited extent against college freshman and lightweight crews, Kent built on its reputation for turning out fine oarsmen. A New England Interscholastic Rowing Association (NEIRA) championship was established in 1947, and after a competition for eights was introduced in 1950, Kent crews won better than half of them over the next twenty years. (In fact the trophy for the victor ultimately became known as the Sill Cup.) Kent even had its first Olympic representative when William Stowe, class of 1958, stroked his Vesper Boat Club (Philadelphia) to a gold medal at the 1964 Olympics in Tokyo.

As Tote Walker contemplated retirement in the early 1960s, he decided to bring on a talented young assistant who had been coaching the Dartmouth varsity lightweight crew for several years. William Hartwell Perry Jr. had even managed to find the time to coach rowing at the Iolanni School in Honolulu while stationed in Hawaii with the Coast Guard in the mid 1950s. Perry became head coach at Kent in 1964,[*] and was given an experienced oarsman to build his program around the following year when a man of a boy, Fred Schoch, enrolled at the school. Schoch just happened to be the son of the head coach at Princeton and had grown up around the sport. (The elder Schoch, known as Dutch, was a spare on the University of Washington crew that won gold in front of Adolf Hitler at the 1936 Olympics.) It's not clear whether Perry actively recruited Schoch or that his father merely thought Kent would be the best place to nurture his son's rowing talent. But in Schoch Perry had a young man of considerable size and skill with the potential to be a true leader.

When I enrolled at Kent in the fall of 1968, Fred Schoch was something of an iconic figure to us freshmen and sym-

---

[*] For those keeping score, Kent had by now had more headmasters than crew coaches.

bolized all the gravitas and tradition of the Kent School Boat Club. My classmates Fred Elliott, Murray Beach, Geoff O'Keefe, Roger Stewart, and Garth Griffin may have day-dreamed about someday being a part of that tradition, but I certainly did not. For me, achieving such athletic heights constituted nothing short of the Herculean effort and talent for luck of a moon shot. I saw Fred and his fellow oars-men as completely beyond reach, towering athletes who performed on a completely different level than anyone else in any other sport, privileged men who rowed on the most up-to-date equipment and who got to go to places like Eng-land. I had other things to be concerned about, such as just keeping up academically.

I had, after all, enrolled at Kent one year after I should have, a stumble that ironically worked to my advantage just a few short years later.

IV

CLASS OF '72

"If you can dream—and not make dreams your master . . . You'll be a Man my son!"
—RUDYARD KIPLING, "IF"

Take a year, any year, and you could probably write a book making the case that it was the symbolic quintessence of all preceding years or the harbinger of the historical events that would inform those succeeding. Certainly, our history is a staked plain of iconic years that help us find our way from triumph to calamity and back again; 1865, 1898, 1917, 1929, 1945, and 1968 come immediately to mind. In fact, for my generation 1968 was pivotal in that every day, it seemed, another thread in the tapestry of the Republic would come undone, and that one morning we would wake up to find it entirely disassembled. Assassination, war (and the press that turned against it), race riots, and general social unrest played out against the background of traditional American values that were desperately trying to hold the center.

By 1972, however, the forces for change as well as those for moderation seem to have worn themselves out. Much of the so-called counterculture had started to become mainstream: The tribal love-rock musical *Hair,* for example, with its infamous display of naked bodies, had just celebrated its fourth successful year on Broadway, and its melodies had even made their way on to *The Ed Sullivan Show* and Muzak. (Fittingly, however, at a party at the Four Seasons in New York to celebrate the anniversary of the show, thirteen Black Panther protesters and the show's coauthor, Jim Rado, were arrested for disturbing the peace and marijuana use.) For our parents, whose lives had largely been informed by economic depression, war, and institutionalized racial segregation, the changes to our culture were nothing short of revolutionary and not always unwelcome, particularly those regarding civil rights. Their Rubicon was what I call the Spencer Tracy Moment in the film *Guess Who's Coming to Dinner?*, when Tracy's character, in a speech also meant as an homage to his decades-long affair with Katharine Hepburn, declares that he will not stand in the way of his daughter's marriage to a black man. Although the film seems painfully dated today, the fact that it was so popular in its time spoke to the wholesale transformation people like my parents had to make when it became their turn to be the stewards of society. And like all such intellectual odysseys, the journey is often far more interesting than the destination and fraught with personal Sirens that tempted them toward danger in even the most tender moments of their lives.

Shortly after my great-grandmother's death in 1958, my parents moved us out of the city and into Fairfield County, Connecticut. Though there were three of us children now (my brother having been born the previous year) and our Manhattan apartment was no doubt closing in on us, I've never been entirely convinced that the timing was coincidental. Despite being the firstborn son, my father was very much treated as an afterthought by my grandfather,* who much favored the boy from his second marriage. (My uncle Stan never shared his father's grudge and looked up to my father through his entire life. Dad, in kind, always viewed Stan as a true brother.) To move away physically from his father was no doubt an attempt to move away emotionally, and when he quit the Rinehart company (and commuting to its offices in New York) after it morphed into Holt, Rinehart & Winston a few years later, that may have been the exclamation point at the end of a statement that may well have started with the words *Screw you,* if I had had the opportunity to write it then.

But if he was that angry, he contained it in a sense of decorum whose fulcrum was the conviction that one should take care not to speak ill of others. Early on I was to know what it was like to be circumspect in expressing one's

---

* Making matters worse, Dad lived with his severely alcoholic mother most of the time. So concerned was his older sister for his well-being that she turned down the opportunity to be the first woman in our family to attend college to help Dad get through some difficult years.

views, a habit of restraint that was to both hurt me and help me later in life. He was always unfailingly polite, diplomatic, and well spoken. He was also an enchanting raconteur, and even his most apocryphal stories drew calls for an encore. For three children under the age of ten, it was like having a combination of Victor Borge and Bobby McFarrin in the house, since a good story would surely include sound effects, following which you might be treated to the Chiquita Banana song, complete with an imagined pile of fruit carefully balanced on one's head.

Still, for all his talent, my father always seemed to have difficulty holding down a job, mostly because he was unable to identify any sort of métier until much later in life. He did manage a ten-year-long stint at something called the Famous Writer's School in Westport, but once it was discovered that the instructors were neither famous nor necessarily published writers, the end to the enterprise came quickly. Following that, Dad picked up freelance editorial work, got involved in a failed business venture, and spent many a night sipping bourbon and staring at the typewriter hoping something publishable would come out of it. It never did.

If my father was vocationally challenged, though, he enthusiastically filled his time as a serial hobbyist, whether it was building his own stereo (and later, our first color TV), learning to bake bread, painting still lifes, or helping us with our model airplanes. And he didn't need much for inspiration: One night when I was about five or six and couldn't sleep, I came downstairs to discover that Dad had spent the evening building an Indian village, its miniature tepees constructed from toothpicks and adding machine tape. On another occasion he had taken a pile of scrap balsa wood, tissue, and model airplane dope and, from scratch, had constructed a plane with a round wing. It was a beautiful thing to behold, but once it was determined that level flight was impossible—it would corkscrew through the air—he painted his name in Japanese over the wing and hung it over his desk next to a horseshoe crab carcass that he had spray-painted gold. Other oddities in his atelier included his portrait of a young girl rendered on a section of 4x4 post and covered in chicken wire.

But Dad's obsession—it can fairly be called that—was music, in all its richness and forms. Every weekend the house was filled with music from his stereo, Dad often "air conducting" some masterpiece from an imagined podium in the living room. And he taught us everything he knew about music and encouraged us all to take up an instrument or two. Alas, except for two miserable years hacking away at a violin, I never developed the discipline to master an instrument, but I became a decent listener and with my father's guidance learned how to pull apart the braids of a fugue, to give one example. He also had a metronome set up to help us understand tempo, and after a while my sense of rhythm became intuitive, later reflected in the stroke count of an eight-oared shell being rowed to near perfection.

Notwithstanding my father's eccentricities—and probably because of them—my parents were a popular couple. My mother made friends quickly, and because she was a beautiful, outgoing young woman, she attracted many of the male variety. There seemed to be a cocktail party somewhere every weekend, after which my parents would somehow find their way home, since, at least in my father's case, alcohol was starting to become a real problem. If the party was at our house, I often found myself navigating my way around the drunks just to get to the kitchen, while some musical piece that Dad had just discovered blared from the stereo accompanied by his running commentary. Relief would finally come as the noise level dropped some time after midnight, and I knew the house would be ours again when Dad took to his perch on the split-rail fence by the driveway with his guitar to serenade the departing guests with Woody Guthrie's "So long, It's Been Good to Know You."

Although throughout his life my father would never reveal his party affiliation or even so much as whom or what he had voted for, it's pretty clear that both of my parents were fond of JFK and had completely bought into the optimism that his presidency meant. They also started to get caught up in the changing politics of the 1960s, supporting politicians who opposed the war in Vietnam and who advocated the guarantee of civil rights for all. When John F. Kennedy was assassinated in November 1963, my father retreated to his workbench in the garage with a six-pack of beer and his eldest son on the day of the funeral. The service played from a small transistor radio that he had slipped into the pocket of his flannel shirt as he showed me how to build a wren house from some scrap wood. When Gabriel Faure's "Requiem" came on, he sang all the tenor parts, which he knew by heart. Finally, when the service ended with taps, he broke into tears.

For many the Kennedy assassination meant the end of innocence and the beginning of a period of divisive bitterness for the country. And so, too, in the Rinehart household. My parents' medium of communication increasingly became the bicker, making the three children uncomfortable and forcing us to either escape it or try to unsuccessfully mediate our parents' disputes. My father was starting to drink heavily, often disappearing mysteriously at night, and was increasingly moody—but never violent. When I would try to talk to him about his drinking, he would become angry with me. Still, this was the same father who when in sobriety would teach me about everything from gun safety to safe sex (which in those days meant no sex). I was starting to see that Dad was becoming what we all tend to become; that is, many different men.

When I turned fourteen he said something to me that he had intended as a compliment, although I took it as a statement of abandonment at first. "I'm done with you," he told me, the drink no doubt informing his sentiment. "I've done all I can. The rest is up to you." What he had meant, and what I didn't get, was that I had successfully emerged from childhood. And physically, yes, I had, shooting up to about five-foot-eight, although I had never mastered my body to do any sport well, and my newfound height only made me that much more awkward. But emotionally, there was still the vestige of the child in me, so I was hurt by his words.

Still, I was ready to move on, if only to get away from what was an increasingly uncomfortable family situation. My sister had already gone up to Kent, which made me envious in each and every way. My parents also sensed that it was my time to go, and we started looking at suitable boarding schools. However, because of my mediocre grades—both my brother and sister were perennial honor students—the types of schools that I qualified for seemed to be the kinds of places parents sent their children to get rid of them. They all seemed to be at the end of some impossibly long, dark rural road miles from civilization and have campuses with all the charm of a medium-security penitentiary. I wanted to go to a place that was full of light and hope, a school that could somehow awaken my somnolent spirit. I wanted to go to Kent.

So we changed strategy. I would repeat eighth grade at my present school to try to improve my grades. It was humiliating, but because I had not been a complete academic washout, I was still able to take a few classes with my peers. And I enjoyed suddenly finding my name on the honor role.

It worked. On a beautiful spring day in 1968 I went to Kent for my formal tour and interviews. If the admissions department had a plan afoot to recruit me, and there is no reason to believe they did, it could not have been better scripted. I was guided around campus by an upperclassman who seemed genuinely proud of the place, and as we made our way from building to building, my jaded memory recalls, I saw nothing but confidence in the faces of the students. Since my experience with the opposite sex had been somewhat limited—I had been attending an all-boys school—the presence of girls, and apparently hundreds of them, filled me with a sense of expectation that started as a swell in the chest cavity and then headed south to tease an appendage I once thought to be merely vestigial. The day was capped with my first view of crews taking to the water, a different sort of beauty that was nearly as breathtaking as the presence of all those girls.

While I took my tour, my parents gathered with Sid Towle to discuss finances, should I be accepted. No doubt goaded by my grandparents, who would now be footing the bill for two Kent tuitions, my father inquired about the school's famous sliding-scale tuition policies, in search of if not a twofer then a discount. Notwithstanding what must have been a bravura display of charm by my father, Towle was quick with a polite explanation that, sorry, people like you don't qualify for assistance. Understandably so— Towle was only aware of the pedigree, and not my father's record of chronic underemployment. In retrospect it must have taken an awful lot of courage for my parents to even broach the subject, knowing that rejection was an almost laughable inevitability.

In the weeks that followed my visit to Kent, another inevitability happened, a letdown and a doomful sense that I wouldn't get in. My backup plan was to apply to two other schools, only one of which could be called an equal to Kent academically, but more desperately, neither of my backups was coeducational. Having grown up around the same small group of girls in Fairfield County, and failing to really click with any of them, I badly wanted a new social milieu. In more ways than one, I needed to start over again.

So when I was finally accepted at Kent it was with a great sense of relief. It was also the first time I had ever set a goal for myself and achieved something I very much wanted.

The whole process, from visiting those dismal campuses of third-rate schools to swallowing my pride and repeating a grade, was, as politicians like to say, a teachable moment. It also gave me the confidence to reach again for the seemingly unattainable four years later.

In a classic example of not being careful about that for what you wish, when I was deposited* on the Kent campus in September 1968 I found myself utterly friendless and clueless. Since the girl's campus was five miles away atop Skiff Mountain, my sister might as well have been on the moon.

---

* Quite literally. As soon as my bags and I were out of the car, my father shook my hand and left immediately.

(Girls and boys were kept away from each other until classes started.) But Kent had a good system for indoctrinating unwitting third formers, and that was to assign each one a senior (sixth former) sponsor to help them find their way during the first few weeks of school. And my sister, though impaired by distance, had arranged for a good one for me: senior prefect Dick Shell, an effervescently outgoing Adonis (or so my mother thought) who had arrived shell-shocked on the campus four years before, and who now ran the place. (My mother and I always thought that my sister, Deb, and Dick would make a fine couple, but alas, it was never to be, though Dick has remained a great friend to us all over the years.)

After about a week of the usual homesickness, the third formers started to form the kind of bond that comes from unrelenting, and apparently unchecked, hazing by upperclassmen. (Interestingly, the worst of it seemed to come from a group of sadists led by the nephew of a Central American dictator.) But by knowing what hallways to avoid, who not to talk smack to, and, conversely, whose ass to kiss, navigating the campus without getting hung up by one's underwear every day became increasingly possible. And I had yet another foil: the friendship of one of the wittiest of the new boys, Ric Burwell, who would be my roommate for most of our remaining years at Kent. Burwell, as we called him, seemed to be able to wisecrack his way out of any dilemma, and entertained by doing dead-on impersonations of several of the more eccentric faculty.

At first daunting, class work became manageable, especially for someone who feared getting an A as much as
a D and was content to hang out in that middle range of
academic mediocrity. Although I can't recall any course
that you would call ordinary, one stood out above all others: Father Pete Woodward's religion class. Nominally an
Episcopalian, my most recent church education had been
with the Unitarians, who, as H. L. Mencken once observed,
believe God is a Boy Scout. Father Pete redirected my
thinking to the imitation of Christ, and I have never been
the same since.

Mandatory attendance at chapel four times a week
took some getting used to, though it eventually served its
intended purpose of providing a venue and ritual for medi-
tation. It was the service of adoration that was most likely
to move me to pluck petals from my daisy of faith—"He
loves me, He loves me not"; "I believe (in God), I don't
believe"; and so forth. Kneeling on the cold stone of St.
Joseph's while Father Pete defrocked himself in the hazy
glow of candlelight and incense, my imaginary pile of petals was evidence that the man and his teaching were getting to me. Although it would take years before the debate
over faith was ever settled in my mind, the fact that there
was a debate at all was a startling new development.

Often falsely described as isolated and out of touch
with the real world, whatever that was, I found Kent to be
in full stride with the pivotal events of 1968. After class
hours the music of revolution filled the courtyard outside

my window in Middle Dorm; to this day hearing anything by the Doors or Richie Havens instantly takes me back there. Although the controversial election of 2000 has surpassed any previous presidential contest in terms of both excitement and controversy, the Nixon-Humphrey tilt of November 1968 also went down to the wire, and sent us to bed on election night with no knowledge of who our next president was going to be. I so remember Richard Boulware, one of a handful of black students in those days, bursting from his room at 6:30 in the morning following Election Day, demanding to know from any reliable source who the new president was. Once informed that his man, Hubert Humphrey, had lost, he slipped quietly back into his room, his stooped shoulders a picture of despondency.

With both my sister and me now away from home the family dynamic was set for another sea change. One development could have been foretold by anyone: Depending on how you looked at it, my brother was now reaping the rewards, or bearing the brunt, of being an only child. Another change was not so obvious at first: My mother started playing an increasingly larger role in my life, becoming the reliable go-to parent on everything from money to issues with girls. It was almost as if my father had passed me off to her after his famous declaration that he was "done" with me. Though I sensed no malice, looking back on it I am reminded that in business the definition of a successful partnership is that partners are rarely equal all of the time. Ultimately, my parents were unsuccessful in marriage but successful in parenting because where one withdrew, the other knew to take up the slack.

So it was not surprising that the go-to parent was the one who showed up for parents weekend that fall, and who set out a challenge to me that I found so absurd on the face of it that I laughed it off. Sitting in chapel that Sunday morning she happened to notice Fred Schoch and several members of the Kent School Boat Club wearing their "Henley blazers," coats in the manner of the English schoolboy or university oarsman, handsome, dark blue affairs distinguished by gray piping and an elaborate rendition of the Kent seal over the pocket. "What is *that?*" she hissed in a whisper while giving Fred the once over. After I explained to her that the jacket was something Kent oarsmen earned by competing at the Henley Royal Regatta, she let this information sink in a bit before declaring, "I want *you* to get one of *those.*"

The first strike against that ever happening came the following spring when I opted for tennis over crew as my sport of choice. Fortunately for my mother, I completely washed out in the sport and went on to an ignominious but amusingly diverse athletic career for much of my time at Kent. As a reporter for the school paper once noted in a profile, I had tried everything, à la George Plimpton, and excelled at nothing: hockey, lacrosse, basketball, skiing, soccer, and cross-country, to name few, and all exclusively no higher than the club level. "If there's a sport at Kent," the reporter concluded, "then Rick has clubbed it."

The following year, my fourth form year, with the same "what the hell, why not?" approach I had taken with other sports, I decided to try rowing. It had actually all started over the winter, when I snuck out one night afterhours to try a turn on the rowing practice tanks in the basement of one of the classroom buildings. (Imagine a small swimming pool with riggers, oars, and a sliding seat mounted on one side and you've got the idea of a tank.) Very soon after my first few strokes, I was busted by an upperclassman known to be a strict disciplinarian, and I thought I was instantly doomed to spend a month of Saturday nights in study hall. Much to my relief, he decided instead to give me a pass on my curfew violation, and because he was a member of KSBC, he proceeded to coach me on my "technique." Taking the seat in front of me, we rowed together for the better part of an hour, a session during which I got the basics down and learned how important, and, difficult, it was to be precisely synchronous with another oarsman. But the message that I came away with from my lesson in the tanks was that I was coachable.

My first crew that spring was a club third boat, not exactly the right rung of the ladder to be on at the age of sixteen to attain the Henley jacket, but certainly good enough for a first-year oarsman. We won all of our races that year easily, and I started to build a little confidence that I could do this sport. I was also starting to reach the height and weight that I would have for the rest of my prime adult years, and gradually came to the conclusion that if I could avoid tripping myself up with my big feet, I might be able to do something with my long arms and legs.

Hart Perry started to take notice of me as well, but not necessarily for anything having to do with the sport of rowing. Perry was also dean of boys during my time, so as much as I might have been intimidated by him as the current rowing mastermind, I could not escape his radar as the school's lead disciplinarian. During my four years at Kent I had my fair share of encounters with him on the wrong side of the disciplinary divide, most notably during my fifth form year when I seemed to be slipping from Kent's narrow beam of discipline. (Among other things, I had initiated a beer party on a Kent-bound train and had got caught smoking in a dorm room.) His response to these indiscretions was counterintuitive but wholly effective: He placed me on a disciplinary committee, where I would sit in judgment of other students' indiscretions, and he suggested I start working out with the school's "serious" oarsmen. In other words, start running with a different crowd and take a stab at making the KSBC. Alas, I arrived for the spring break practices about ten pounds overweight, stuffed myself some more at the training table, and failed to make the cut. While my technique was fine, most everything else was not. Hart allowed as to how I might be a spare for his second boat if someone should get sick or injured, and then sent me back to the clubs. He suggested that I do something over the summer to "toughen up," like an Outward Bound course.

The exile to club rowing turned out to be a godsend; while Perry's first and second crews had an average year, my boat, a first club boat, tore up the Housatonic with a piratelike swagger. Composed of would-bes and wannabes—several of my fellow oarsman could have easily made KSBC but chose to forgo the huge commitment that it involved—we were driven by a bulldog of a coach, Mr. Gaston, who refused to remember our names and added further injury to the insult by making something up. (For some reason I was Rinebolt.) The only way to get even with the man was to win boat races, and this we did by sweeping all of our intramural races, beating a couple of B-level boarding school first boats, and taking KSBC's own second. Another year on the waters, another year undefeated.

I did take Perry up on his suggestion that summer and headed to Colorado for a monthlong Outward Bound course, bracketed at both ends by putting in some time at a ranch stacking hay bales. By this time I knew I had a reasonable shot at making the KSBC second boat the following spring; adding further motivation to make the club was the fact that I had been tapped as a prefect for my sixth form year, and club sports is not part of that résumé. So I hit the Colorado mountains determined to lose the last vestige of baby fat and find out where my physical limit was.

It turns out that my limit was apparently six inches of water in a mountain streambed at about 8,000 feet. Called upon with two others to arrange for the rescue of an injured climber in our patrol, our charge was to hike twenty miles or so on a moonlit night above timberline to seek out a University of Colorado research camp. Once there, we would awaken the scientists and have them drive us into Silverton to call for help. All went as planned, and we were able to rest briefly in Silverton (though on wooden church pews) until we received word that we were to hike back to our base camp. This was the equivalent of nearly fifty miles of hiking over a sixteen-hour period with little, if any, sleep. Still, we soldiered on ably, at least until the encounter with the stream. While my mates skillfully hopped on rocks to avoid getting wet, for some reason, probably exhaustion, I chose the path of least resistance and slogged right through the water. Within minutes my feet were prunes, and very painful ones at that. Urging my comrades to proceed without me, I pretty much crawled all the way back to camp, delusional and probably suffering from the initial stages of exposure. But I had made it.

After a month of hiking in the San Juans, our Outward Bound course concluded with a half-marathon through the mountains, though since political correctness was just starting to rear its ugly head, there were to be no "winners" or "losers" among the 150 or so participants, just "finishers." (In addition to its physical challenges, Outward Bound in those days also offered an indoctrination into utopian socialism.) Like all such naive ideals, though, this one quickly died when confronted with reality, as about fifty of us bolted from the start to make it a race. Much to my surprise, I finished third.

Though unquestionably fitter than I had been at any time in my life, I was taken down again that summer by an amoeba after I had inadvertently taken water from an irrigation ditch frequented by cows. My weight dropped some twenty pounds before I returned to Kent in September, and it took nearly six months to put it all back on.

The fall of 1971 brought a mixed bag of changes and some new concerns. On September 30 I turned eighteen, which meant, on the one hand, that I could have a beer in New York State, a short drive from Kent. On the other hand, I was now eligible for the draft with a war still festering in Southeast Asia. Although U.S. troop levels in Vietnam were down to about 200,000 soldiers at the time of my birthday, and the next draft lottery was not scheduled until February 1972, getting a low number would surely cause an unwelcome disruption in my life whether I enlisted in the army or not. As my parents floated various schemes such as having me escape to Canada or pressuring their local congressman to grant me some kind of exemption, I struggled with the notion of dodging the draft on its face. The war was of course very unpopular and had nearly brought the Republic to its knees, but is that any reason to refuse to serve your country? This was the conundrum that I had to live with until the situation ultimately resolved itself five months later.

The challenge of whether or not to accept my fate if the lottery did not go my way was eased by a development of the most surprising kind: By the middle of the semester I had fallen in love with a spirited girl by the name of Liz Pegram and she, apparently, with me. While I had dated several Kent girls over the years, these relationships always managed to fizzle out by the time school ended for the year. But this one was different. Liz—blond, athletic, and a kind of Mistress Quickly of Kent School—was a keeper. She was at ease with adults and quickly won over my parents. My parents then befriended her mother and her boyfriend, and the foursome became almost as inseparable as Liz and I had. After just a few short months we all had a sense that we were in it for the long haul. Indeed, Liz and I discreetly reaped what the sexual revolution had sewn, and with a sort of unspoken acknowledgment of our parents. It is ironic but perfectly understandable that we were free to act as normal adults away from Kent, so we spent many a weekend away—at least until crew season—enjoying ourselves and, yes, even the company of our parents.

The distractions of love and war notwithstanding, that winter I completely dedicated myself to rowing, leveraging my status as a sixth former and prefect to skip the traditional winter sports and just train with other oarsmen. A new machine called an ergometer was installed in the boathouse, a no-nonsense device that literally measured strength and quickly separated the men from the boys. After a few scary turns on the machine, I found that my strength was nicely average, neither the weakest of all the KSBC candidates nor the strongest. Thanks, perhaps, to that fifty-mile hike in Colorado, I also found that I could sustain my strength just long enough to complete a mock boat race. And I knew it would all just get better once I finally got over the dysentery.

I was also now able to concentrate a mind unfettered with concern about my future: In February the draft lottery had been held, and my number came in well above the cut-off for draft-eligible eighteen-year-olds at 110.

By the time the ice was starting to break up on the Housatonic in the late winter of 1972, I was pretty confident about making KSBC's second, or junior varsity, boat. As added insurance, perhaps, I had followed Hart Perry's advice and befriended a number of the KSBC veterans—Murray Beach, Fred Elliott, and Charlie Poole in particular. Murray, the clear favorite to become captain and stroke of the first boat, was a natural leader, a serious, hardworking oarsman thoroughly dedicated to the sport. Fred Elliott was thin and light but pound for pound the strongest oarsman Kent had. Charlie Poole was a big fellow with a great rowing pedigree; his brother, Malcolm, was a key man on Fred Schoch's boat in 1969.

This was the core group that sacrificed its spring break that year to form the two crews that would represent Kent. Among the two dozen or so other candidates were two promising underclassmen, Charlie Kershaw and Clint Whistler; another returning first boat oarsman, Geoff O'Keefe; an athlete originally recruited to Kent for hockey, John Rooney; and a big man from the previous year's second boat, Mike "Pa"* Brown, who was recovering from a broken wrist. Except for Murray at stroke, Geoff somewhere on the starboard side, and Roger Stewart as coxswain, it was an open competition in both boats for any and all seats. And the vacancies were many: Not only did Perry have to fill an entire second eight with oarsmen elevated from the clubs, but the first boat had at least four seats up for grabs as well. While it was generally believed that the 1971 first eight had underachieved, KSBC had still lost an eight's worth of outstanding oarsmen through graduation and attrition. The 1972 crews looked to be among the least experienced in years.

Still, Hart Perry was not going to let any of us use that as an excuse for mediocrity. In a memo to us prior to the beginning of two-a-day practices on March 24 (we had actually been rowing since March 11, as soon as the Housatonic was ice-free), he reminded us that "we have a wonderful tradition to uphold this year and to do so requires desire, hard work, and pride in the highest possible degree." He continued, "Each man has to give of himself willingly and whole heartedly to the extent he is in *perfect* condition. No one oarsman can ride in the boat with seven others trying to take up the slack. Think carefully—if you have *any* doubts as to your dedication and selflessness, Kent crew is *not* your sport."

In his marvelous book on four oarsmen preparing for the 1984 Olympics, *The Amateurs,* David Halberstam refers to

---

* So called, apparently, for his deep Southern drawl.

the rowing community as a "closed one" in which "rivalries and jealousies were greatly magnified." A "critical part of the bond" among competing oarsmen was, according to Halberstam, accepting what he called the Pain. Men of "lesser will and ambition" simply did not make the cut. Rowing engages nearly every muscle in the body, and in a race that means stressing all of them to the maximum for five to ten minutes.* To further elaborate on the significance of the Pain, Halberstam goes on to give examples of legendary oarsmen passing out after a race or even just a session on an ergometer. So when Hart Perry wrote of "dedication and selflessness," he was really talking about the Pain.

One of the first combinations Perry tried had me at the number three (or gimp seat†) position on the first boat, but I was viewed as a placeholder for Brown while his wrist recovered. In time it was expected that I would be back on the second boat, probably at the number seven position. Still, as Hart moved others in and out of the first boat, I remained at three, then later, bow. Eventually he settled on a lineup that consisted of me, Kershaw, Elliott, Rooney, O'Keefe, Whistler, Poole, and Beach from bow to stern. Once Pa Brown had healed, it was understood, he could challenge for my position.

Roger Stewart's log entries, like a palimpsest, reveal how the boat evolved over two weeks. His daily commen-

---

* It is said that rowing a 2,000-meter race is the physiological equivalent of playing back-to-back basketball games.

† The position, as the glossary to this book describes it, with the "least responsibility."

tary with me in the gimp seat and various others moving in and out of the boat was at first pretty discouraging:

> *March 12: Finishes horrible. Slides very rushed.*
> *March 16: Rotten.*
> *March 25: Horrible timing . . . inexperience in both boats showed.*
> *March 26: Worthless.*

On March 27 I made the move to bow and Fred Elliott took over at three. Charlie Kershaw was brought over from the second boat to fill the number two seat. The difference was felt almost immediately:

> *March 27: It's pulling together . . . settles and sprints not bad . . . [the crew] pulled the boat together beautifully.*
> *March 28 (We were now practicing with Dartmouth): Went two two-minute pieces with Dartmouth Freshmen heavies. Walked on 'em—at least 3 lengths open [water] every time.*
> *March 29: Rhythm is coming nicely.*
> *March 30: Flying.*
> *March 31: We're ready for Yale . . .*

It clearly helped our quick development that we had a brand-new, state-of-the-art eight to row, christened the *Frederick Herbert Sill* in recognition of fifty years of rowing at Kent. A creation of Helmut Schoenbrod's, it featured, for the first time, track shoes bolted into the stretchers to keep our feet secured rather than the usual Roman-era looking leather straps. Measuring fifty-eight feet in length and designed for a crew averaging 175 pounds, it may also have been one of the last great wooden racing shells ever built. While previous Schoenbrod boats had a reputation for being unstable, the breakthrough design of the *Sill* with its more rounded hull gave it, as one oarsman put it, a rocklike

Our formal team photo. From left to right: John Menge, the author, Charlie Kershaw, Fred Elliott, John Rooney, Roger Stewart *(crouching)*, Geoff O'Keefe, Clint Whistler, Charlie Poole, Murray Beach, and Hart Perry. *Author's Collection.*

stability. A native of Germany, Schoenbrod's boats also had the European influence of lighter but stronger construction. More advanced carbon-fiber versions of the *Sill* came to dominate collegiate rowing for the next half decade. Important for me, I was right at the boat's optimal average weight at 175 pounds, and at six-foot-one I had a decent reach. The *Sill* was designed for a tall bowman to stretch out and raise the bow, thus minimizing drag.

I don't recall any great moment of celebration at having made the first boat, and my mother certainly didn't start booking flights for London when I did. Since the 1971 first boat had gone to Henley and lost in the first heat, it was pretty clear that we'd have to run the table in the United States to merit a return trip. That seemed highly improbable. We were young and inexperienced and had a hockey player in the number four position, for heavens' sake. Our number six man had just turned sixteen, and the fellow in the bow was still recovering from amoebic dysentery. And the looming presence of people like Pa Brown was a constant reminder that if we faltered in our first couple of races, any one of us could be replaced at any time.

V

BOYS OF SPRING

"If the boat is really working perfectly . . . you don't feel conscious of other people. You feel more conscious of your own strength through seven other people. When the boat goes perfectly, I feel it's because of me."

—STEVE KIESLING, *THE SHELL GAME*

Our first test, such as it was, came on April Fools' Day against a Yale freshman heavyweight boat on our mile-long home course. It was more or less a preseason race that Perry and the Yale coach had arranged at the last minute, prelude to our formal debut seven days later against Yale and Coast Guard varsity lightweights on the Yale course at Derby, Connecticut. The Yale freshmen heavies proved not to be much of a challenge, nor did we learn much about ourselves as we cruised to a win of four lengths. Again as a warm-up, the following Monday we hosted and raced an English crew said to be among the top ten in Britain, Bryanston, which we beat by sixteen seconds. At a reception following the race, Sid Towle told the assembled that if we went undefeated that spring we'd return to England to challenge for the Princess Elizabeth Cup. Most of us looked at him with incredulity.

————

Of all the positions on an eight, that of coxswain is probably the loneliest and most thankless. Although at first blush
it would appear that the cox has only two jobs—to steer
the boat and bark out commands, all the while enjoying a
fine ride on the water—such an impression belies the many
responsibilities of the coxswain both on and off the water.
During a race a cox is by turns a coach, navigator, and
cheerleader. Since his eight oarsmen are rowing with their
backs to the bow and concentrating on the man in front of
them, the coxswain is also the eyes of the boat. He or she
must tell the crew where it is in relation to other boats,
usually by shouting his own position relative to that of a
seat on an opposing boat. "I have *two!*" for example, would
mean that he is opposite the number two man. His job in
looking downriver is made all the more difficult because
he has eight large oarsmen blocking his vision. However,
if he has prepared properly he has probably surveyed the
course thoroughly prior to the race and perhaps even made
a sketch of it.

Along with the stroke, the oarsman directly in front
of him who sets the pace for the seven other oarsmen, the
coxswain manages a race by calling for "leg drives" (more
power), upping or decreasing the stroke count, or initiating
a sprint, if needed, as the boat nears the finish line. Since
rowing is one of those sports where the coach can't call a
time-out to send in a play, or more appropriately change

strategy, the interplay of the cox and stroke is crucial to a successful crew.

On land the coxswain is responsible for maintaining the boat and its equipment. On certain crews he can also serve as something of a valet for his oarsmen—in fact, *coxswain* may be derived from the Middle English *cox* (small boat) plus *swain* (servant). He can, in certain circumstances, be responsible for everything from the crews' laundry to what goes on the training table. Because coxswains are the jockeys of rowing and as such have to be mindful of their weight, watching eight brawny oarsmen down a meal can be downright agonizing.

Coxswains suffer a further humility even in victory: Tradition holds that a winning crew punctuates its victory by ceremoniously tossing their coxswain in the water, no matter what the temperature. As recounted by Benjamin Ivry in his book *Regatta,* the diminutive British actor Dudley Moore was once asked why he never coxed for Magdalene College, Oxford, while he was a student there. "If you win," Dudley replied, "you get tossed into the water. If you lose, you get beaten up at 3 a.m. by eight burly blokes."

Our coxswain, Roger Stewart, didn't quite fit the physical mold for the position. At nearly five-foot-eight he could easily have hung 140 pounds on his frame and still looked trim; as it was he had to practically starve himself every week to get into the boat at 110 pounds by race time on Saturday. His logs from that year are replete with references to food, both good and bad. Typical of his obsession with food was this entry describing a trip to Philadelphia: "I was so hungry. I remember stopping at the Howard Johnson's—the guys [oarsmen] bought hamburgers and they looked so good. The expensive chocolate chip cookies looked *mmm*." And later just this random comment: "I hate lettuce." He got through most weeks on a diet of toast and tea, then allowed himself a proper meal Saturday night following a race and on Sunday. On Monday it was back to the toast and tea. Starving and binging had become his equivalent of the Pain. He claims to this day that his dieting forever altered his metabolism, and not in a good way. And he still hates lettuce.

Roger's other physical challenge every week was to not shout himself hoarse. In time coxswains would be mic'd with small speakers distributed through the boat so that commands could be given in a normal speaking voice,* but in 1972 the most common amplifying device was a small megaphone fitted to a head brace, freeing up the cox's hands for steering. For his commands to reach me nearly fifty feet away in the bow required a fair amount of controlled hollering. So during the week he added lozenges to his skimpy diet of toast and tea.

Keeping the equipment properly stored and maintained was something else that might have kept him up at night. Because the riggers were removed every day after practice and stored directly above the overturned hull of the shell, he was haunted by visions of one or all of them crashing

---

* Inelegantly known as a "cox box," sophisticated amplification devices may also have digital readouts for stroke counts, speed, and times.

down on the boat and effectively putting it out of commission. He was also obsessed with checking and double-checking slides, riggers, and other moving parts prior to a race. A measure of his anxiety can be found in a log entry from one race in which he wrote that he had "tightened up some bolts checking for what I was scared of—broken equipment. That scared me the most."

To say that these physical and mental challenges would explain why Roger was so tightly wound would be an injustice to someone who was really something of a perfectionist. He was also one of the smartest students in our class, if not the entire school. And he had something of a chip on his shoulder: His brother Lee, whom he idolized, had coxed a Kent Henley crew in 1967. If that were not enough, he had come to Kent his (and my) third-form year directly from Monteria, Colombia, where his parents were Presbyterian missionaries for forty years. He considered himself wholly unprepared to adjust to social life at Kent, although since he and I took French together all four years, the only thing I found odd about him was that he spoke French with a Spanish accent. But Roger was determined to make it work. "My parents took me to show me other schools, including Andover, but I refused," he wrote me. "I wanted Kent."

———————

The 1950 Kent crew, the last crew to go undefeated on both sides of the Atlantic, also started its season with a race with

Yale at Derby. As Jim Young, the number two man on the boat recalls, "The wind whistled behind us and the spring freshet created a rapidly flowing Housatonic River. Waves made the rowing difficult, but the conditions enabled us to fly. We crossed the finish line three-quarters of a length ahead [of Yale] . . . at a record time of 4:52 minutes."

Conditions for our debut race against Yale and Coast Guard on April 8, 1972, were similar and quite possibly worse. In fact, they were about as unfavorable as you can have for rowing. Although the sun was out and the sky glowed a cerulean blue, winter decided to return for a brief encore, raking the lower Housatonic with a fierce, icy wind that caused our hands to crack and bleed as we gripped our sweeps. Common sense also dictated that we row in our warm-ups, which were nothing but and frequently referred to as our cool-downs. Still, anything was better than our skimpy white shorts and T-shirts.

The choppy waves on the river's surface reached nearly half a foot, so that when we swept back to hit the catch there was the occasional jarring *thwack* of an oar blade hitting the crest of a wave—which, of course, would make the boat suddenly lurch to port or starboard. As we practiced 100-meter sets we struggled to keep both ourselves and the *Sill* on an even keel. It was little consolation to us that the opposing crews were having an even harder time keeping their boats under control. When we finally lined up at the start, all I could think about was that I wanted to make a respectable showing and then get the hell out of there. (Of course, I was just about to learn that it's never enough just to make a respectable showing in competition. You compete to win.)

Prior to the race Roger and Murray had gone out on the river and surveyed the 2,000-meter course in detail. Roger sketched a simple but accurate map—which survives to this day—showing the 500-meter intervals, location of buoys, shoreline contours, and even the railroad tracks on the far side of the river. Being aware of what the shoreline was doing in particular was critical in any race, since getting the pull of an eddy, for example, can slow you down.

Notwithstanding the chop, we got off to a clean start at the gun and drove the *Sill* quickly forward at a cadence of forty-three strokes per minute. At first Coast Guard had a slim lead, but they soon faded, making it a race between Kent and Yale. Powering with leg drives to make a move on the Elis, we jumped out to a three-quarter-length lead and kept gaining. Because control was as vital as power in the conditions, it was important to keep our composure, especially when a burst of wind would suddenly pitch the boat to one side. But like a rider who gradually gets a feel for a horse, our hours of practice in the *Sill* gave us an intuitive sense of where we were. We crossed the finish line a full length ahead of Yale and two lengths ahead of Coast Guard.

But it was a short-lived victory. Probably because of the chop, Roger had lost sight of one of the lane markers and inadvertently cut inside of it. While this gave us no particular advantage, rules are rules, and we were disqualified.

Roger was of course devastated and shouldered the entire blame, but the reaction of his eight oarsmen and coach was oddly divided—but not divisive. Those of us who were new to KSBC celebrated it as a win, and an impressive one. (Our competitors tended to agree and magnanimously offered congratulations in spite of the disqualification.)* On the other hand, Murray and Hart Perry were furious with Roger and never let him forget about it throughout the season. I thought that this was unfair until I realized that this was just good coaching. Hart had repeatedly beat into us the trite but necessary words "Winning isn't everything. It's the only thing." Now no one would ever misunderstand what he meant.

Still, the improbable outcome of the race and the impressive margin of victory had taught us something about ourselves. We now knew we were fast. And the disqualification only made us more defiant. We came together as a crew that day. We were no longer eight random oarsmen and a coxswain, but we were Kent's first boat, a band of brothers. Life seldom offers such satisfying moments of self-discovery, but we had just been handed one. Decades later the crew, to a man, would cite the race at Derby as the moment we knew we had the possibility to achieve something extraordinary. I also started to feel inhered with a power that I can't explain to this

---

* Such is the mythology that has grown around the race that in discussing it with John Rooney in an interview for this book, he suddenly stopped me and said, "*What? We were disqualified?*" in complete seriousness.

day, a sense that someone or something was pushing us. Maybe it was just the testosterone, but long after that had lost its effect I would find myself looking out at a blank sky in wonder.

The day following the race, in an article that was supposed to have touted Coast Guard's surprising victory over Yale in the varsity heavyweight race also held that day, a *New Haven Register* reporter instead fell all over himself (and with tortured grammar) to minimize the relevance of our disqualification. "Yale was awarded the victory," he wrote, "but the official outcome didn't fool anyone. . . . [Kent] rowed with poise and precision which would have done honor to their elders. . . . That anyone would row with precision on an afternoon which saw the temperature on the water well below freezing and the water rolling with a heavy chop borne out of a strong downstream wind was hard to believe." He further quoted the Yale lightweight coach as saying flatly, "Kent won the race. They are a very fine crew, particularly when you consider they whipped two college eights." But it was Hart Perry who had the final word: "I'd hate to be the next guys we meet," he muttered drolly as we prepared to depart Derby.

Swing is to rowing what Nirvana is to Buddhism: a perfect state of oarsmanship seemingly free from error. David Halberstam summed up this phenomenon in *The Amateurs:*

When most oarsmen talked about their perfect moments in a boat, they referred not so much to winning a race but to the feel of the boat, all eight oars in the water together, the synchronization almost perfect. In moments like that, the boat seemed to lift right out of the water.

An Olympic oarsman explained to Halberstam what swing really meant to him: "it allowed you to *trust* the other men in the boat. A boat did not have swing unless everyone was putting out in exact measure."

Throughout his rowing career Murray Beach experienced swing many times, but not nearly so quickly as with his 1972 Kent crew. Thirty years later Geoff O'Keefe still marveled at our "wonderful acceleration" and "great swing." John Rooney put it more poetically: There may have been nine men in the boat, but there was "only one soul." Prior to my ascension to the boat, I had experienced such a phenomenon rarely, if at all. It often takes several months for a crew to come together; in the short schoolboy season frequently just as the school year ends and it's time to go home. But we had done it in a matter of a few weeks, and it paid off in the race at Derby. Although conditions made perfection impossible, we had rowed perfectly for the conditions.

Aside from that feel of the boat "lifting" out of the water, there were a couple of other indications of swing for us. Roger would always hear an odd trickle sound

"Swing." Perfect synchronicity. *Author's Collection.*

beneath him when we were performing especially well. Hart Perry would let us know in the most complimentary of ways; other than say something like "moving well" from his launch, he would simply stop coaching and watch us. Who could blame him? It is, after all, one of the moments a person coaches for.

In retrospect it's possible to attribute the fact that we had found our rowing mojo so quickly to a number of factors, luck not being one of them. Rowing is just too difficult a sport for chance to play any role in the success of a crew, especially in an eight where you have the possibility of up to eight different things going wrong. More practically (and obviously) the first thing you do is put the right people in the right positions. In an eight that usually means that your heavier oarsmen occupy the stern four seats with lighter, and perhaps smaller, oarsmen in the bow four. The tallest member of our boat was in the bow for reasons that I have explained, however, and Murray at just about six feet tall and 175 pounds was all the way at the other end at stroke. The two smallest of our oarsmen, Charlie Kershaw and Fred Elliott, were in front of me at the number two and three seats, followed by John Rooney, who weighed in at about 180 pounds. True to form, our biggest men occupied the three remaining stern seats, averaging about 185 pounds each, give or take.

The other factor contributing to the dynamic of the crew is that not only did we have great leadership, we had great "followship" as well. Murray kept his crew in line by, in turn, showing respect where it was warranted and exercising discipline and control where it was needed. He was also uncompromising when it came to competition. We could never win by a large enough margin. The talented but under-achieving crew of the previous year had no such mantra, and indeed had been defeated not so much by outmatched skill as attitude. Long though the odds were for us at the beginning of our season, Murray would practically will us to overcome our doubts about ourselves. Importantly, to a man, we bought into it. As he recently put it, "you really paid attention and kept your heads inside the boat."

Like a number of us, Murray Beach was a legacy whose father and two older brothers had preceded him at Kent. When Murray visited the campus as a child for his father's twentieth reunion, he saw his first crew race. He was immediately taken by the beauty of the sport and the apparent gravitas of KSBC. When it became time for him to choose a school several years later, there was no doubt: Like Roger, he "wanted" Kent. The moment he walked on to the campus in the fall of 1968, he set his sights on the boathouse, though he thought he would play football and wrestle as well. But his athletic career at Kent got off to an unfortunate start when, playing for the third football team, he blocked a punt with his face. The bull's-eye trajectory of the football left him blinded in one eye for a time and ended his football career.

His roommate during most of his years at Kent was Fred Elliott, who described Beach as "far more businesslike than most third formers and [he] seemed to have an advanced grasp on the way Kent operated." Furthermore, "while it never came out during third form year, it was evident that he had his eyes set on becoming a prefect and being a member of KSBC."

Murray's third form year he made a second club boat rowing at the number five position; by the next year he was in the KSBC second boat. In 1971 he rowed in the number two position on the KSBC first boat until the eve of their departure for England, when he was moved to stroke. Given the disappointing record of the crew, it's hard to say whether Hart Perry was looking for answers or looking toward the future.*

---

* Murray again competed internationally that summer as part of a junior pair at the World Championship in Greece. His partner was Tiff Wood, a future Olympian known as "the Hammer" for the ferocity of his stroke. Unfortunately, both oarsmen fell ill and fared poorly at the regatta.

If Murray Beach was all business, Charlie Poole, at times, was comic relief. He seemed to embody not only the stout, hardy New Englander, but also a seemingly insouciant approach to competition born of self-confidence and outright fearlessness. Attach this to a wonderful garrulousness and you have one of the most important players on any athletic team—someone who can loosen you up.

One of five Poole siblings to attend Kent,* Charlie had big shoes to fill when he arrived on campus in the fall of 1969; his older brother Malcolm, who had graduated the previous spring, had been the number five man on the KSBC first boat stroked by Fred Schoch. When word got to Hart Perry that Charlie was leaning toward sailing and not rowing for his spring sport, he found a note on his dorm room door that read something to the effect of: "Come see me at once. WHP." Since Perry was dean of boys, the urgency was ominous. But Charlie hadn't done anything wrong, other than to momentarily derail Perry's plans for him with KSBC. After a conversation that must have been very much one-sided, Charlie left the dean's office an oarsman. He made a third club boat that spring and made the leap to KSBC the following year, earning a seat on the second boat. By 1972, his junior year, he had made it to the number seven seat right behind Murray Beach on the *Sill*.

---

* They were, oldest to youngest: Malcolm, Parker, Charlie, Tina, and Sam. Sam had a bad heart and was taken out of school for a time to have one of the first heart transplants, but didn't survive. His mother, Victoria, wrote a best-selling book about the ordeal, *Wednesday's Child,* which was also made into a movie for TV.

At just about six feet tall, Poole made up in sheer bulk what he may have lacked in height, and his brute strength served him well for many years of heavyweight rowing after he left Kent. He was probably one of the strongest oarsman we had, and his intensity during our early races always had a signature moment when he would drop his head into the boat at the beginning of a finishing sprint, then rise up with the next stroke to give it everything he had. More than one photo from our early races shows the boat going into a sprint with the seven man apparently decapitated. At some point Hart Perry had seen enough, and ordered him to keep his head up at all times.

Where Charlie Poole was a gregarious mensch, the man behind him in the number six position, Clint Whistler, was

Murray Beach and Charlie Poole. *Author's Collection.*

something of a social recluse. The stepson of an Episcopal minister from Illinois—his father had died when he was just a young boy—Clint had clearly lived a sheltered life before arriving at Kent. Only a fourth former and barely sixteen, he and I might as well have been ten years apart rather than the nearly three that separated us. But the differences went deeper: Where I was an unreserved social animal, he would hide in his room if a woman appeared within two hundred yards of his dormitory. And if rumors of our debauching never reached him, he at least knew that I had a girlfriend that I very much enjoyed. This was all unfamiliar territory to him. It was only until many years later that we found out how deeply withdrawn he really was.

On the water, though, Clint was, as Murray described him, a rock. While most boys attain their adult height by the age of sixteen, it can take several years for their musculature to develop. Not so with Clint: He was already there at nearly 180 pounds. Both Hart and Murray saw his potential and decided to make him their project. Whereas I pretty much made up my own workout regimen during the winter of 1971–72, Murray worked with Clint nearly every day. Fortuitously, Murray insisted that Clint master both port and starboard sides of the boat, something I was never once asked to do. In retrospect this turned out to be a brilliant move.

Our number five man, Geoff O'Keefe, was yet another member of the class of 1972 who was inspired by Fred Schoch's 1969 crew—"rowing gods," as he recalled them. Known variously as Charlie, Atlas, and O'Beef, Geoff was known to be a ferociously hard worker both in the classroom and the weight room, and his ripped, almost simianlike physique proved it. He "trained like hell" and made KSBC's second boat his fourth form year. The next year, 1971, he was on the first boat, for which he was rewarded with, as he put it, "a lousy losing season" due to "egos" and "lack of teamwork." After returning from England that summer he vowed to never let that happen again. He worked out in a barn near his home in tiny Vinalhaven, Maine, a town in the Fox Islands known for granite quarries and lobster fisheries and only accessible by ferry. To keep him motivated in his solitary workouts, he wrote his goals on the barn wall in bold marker: "1972 Kent Crew, Undefeated, Stotesbury Cup winners, NEIRA winners, PE Cup winner at Henley-North American schoolboy champions." He checked recently and the words are still there.

In many respects, there is no way that John Rooney should ever have been a member of our crew. For starters, the only rowing experience he had had was on a fourth club boat in 1971. He performed miserably on the ergometer. He was, at times, a hot head with a hair-trigger temper. He talked too much. To demonstrate to the world that he was a hockey player first and an oarsman second, he religiously wore a red ski cap with an annoying tassel that he had been given at a hockey tournament some time before enrolling at Kent. Still, Hart Perry was determined to find a place for him on the first boat even if it meant displacing an oarsman with more experience.

What Perry intuited in Rooney were the kinds of things you can't coach: a fierce competitiveness, a toughness that came from the physical punishment of ice hockey, and a big heart. He might have also sensed that, coming from a lower-middle-class family in suburban Boston, he had something to prove.

John Rooney was just the sort of person Father Sill may have had in mind when he developed the sliding-scale tuition for promising students with limited means. He first caught the eye of Kent's hockey coach, Peter Bragdon, at a tournament in Massachusetts, and when Bragdon learned that John was a decent student as well, saw him as Kent material. He may also have seen something in the character of Rooney's father: a hard-working man who nevertheless

John Rooney, hockey player. *Author's Collection.*

made time for his children by attending each and every game they played.

If John Rooney's placement on the crew may have been, on the surface anyway, improbable, Fred Elliott's may have been destiny. His father, John, had gone to Kent and been senior prefect in 1947, which Fred described as "pretty much all of his formal education." Flunking out of St. Lawrence his freshmen year, John went to work for his father at Elliott Ticket Company, printing such things as 1x2 movie roll tickets, parking lot tags, and restaurant guest checks. Nominally residents of Scarsdale, New York, "technically it was Eastchester," Fred recalled, "middle class" and "struggling." But John had loved Kent and was going to do everything he could to see that Fred would go there. Fred recalls that he first learned to row at the age of five when his father took him out in a dinghy on Long Island Sound. "If you get good at this," John told his son, "when you grow up you might have the chance to row for Kent School."

Fred entered Kent with me in the fall of 1968. His first boat that year was so low on Kent's rowing pecking order that eventually landing on a KSBC boat might indeed have been dreaming the impossible dream. Failing to even make a club fourth boat, he wound up with seven other "misfits" on Kent's fifteenth boat, named *Dinkel's Dingbats* in honor of their patient coach. He can't recall if they even had a race that year. Like a lot of us, though, he was in awe of Fred Schoch and his fine crew and just kept "plugging away." He made a club fourth boat the next year, then made the leap to the KSBC second boat his fifth form year. He traveled to England with the 1971 crew to row in a four not only at Henley but also regattas at Redding and Marlow. Out of that trip came a story that demonstrated the liberties accorded Kent oarsmen while abroad, and how such liberties were to be only discreetly exploited. Following dinner one night before a race, Fred was enjoying a glass of brandy when Sid Towle suddenly turned to him, looked unfavorably at his snifter, and scowled, "Well, as a spare for the varsity now, I hope no one in that boat gets ill tonight."

After getting to know Fred well, it was easy to see the qualities that made him a better than average oarsman. Though relatively light and thin at 160 pounds and measuring just under six feet tall—his almost skeletal profile eventually earned him the sobriquet Bones—Fred made up for his size with his fierce determination. And his intensity was probably only matched by Murray's. As roommates for four years, their passion for the sport no doubt fed off each other. While away from the boathouse Fred was a kind, drolly amusing, and rather low-key all-around good guy, on the water he was a wound spring poised to unleash some serious power.

The man behind Fred in the boat (and ergo, in front of me), Charlie Kershaw (aka Charlie Crewshorts), was the kind of person you'd accidentally leave behind at a truck stop while on a cross-country road trip. He was so low-key that you barely felt his presence. He was also unflappable: He was Dennis Quaid cum Gordon Cooper from *The Right*

Stuff but without the bravado, dealing with an otherwise tense lift-off postponement by sleeping through it. Such a casual demeanor also meant that punctuality was never his strong suit; it seems that when we had to go somewhere we were always waiting for Kershaw. But he was solid in the boat, and as a wrestler brought discipline and coachability to the crew. His small size—he was probably shorter than Roger Stewart—belied his natural strength, affirmed by his success on the wrestling mat. From the moment he was elevated from the second boat, we were a better crew. And his laid-back manner didn't mean that he was at all dismissive of authority; when Hart or Murray spoke, he listened.

Hart Perry's parting words to the *New Haven Register* reporter at Derby proved to be on target; the next Saturday we beat Andover on our home river at Kent by twenty-two seconds, leading from start to finish. Rowing downriver into an intense headwind and lashed by a cold, pelting rain, we nevertheless got off to a smooth start and settled down to a moderate but strong pace. At the quarter-mile marker we were a full length ahead; at the half-mile point it was two lengths. By the finish Andover was over 50 yards to our stern.

As I have previously mentioned, following World War II the sport of rowing started to catch on at high schools in the middle-Atlantic states, and very quickly the competition rose to the level of that of schools like Kent. One of the schools that thoroughly embraced the sport was Washington-Lee High School in Arlington, Virginia, which turned out not only first-rate eights but also sculls, pairs, and fours. Although the program didn't debut until 1949, within a year the Generals, as they were called, had a national champion eight. In 1958 Washington-Lee became the first American public school to compete at Henley (horrors!). By the 1960s the school's incredibly successful rowing program could no longer be ignored, so an annual match race with Kent was established. It quickly became a rivalry that pitted North against South for bragging rights among top schoolboy oarsmen.

The 1971 Kent varsity eight had suffered a bitter defeat to Washington-Lee, so Murray and the other returning oarsmen were clearly out for revenge when we faced them on April 22. They got it. Once again rowing in a cold rain, we got off to a strong start, but after twenty strokes couldn't shake the Generals. After settling down to a pace of thirty-seven strokes per minute, though, we started to pull away. At the halfway point we had a length on them; at the finish the difference was two and a half lengths. Moreover, our time was a very fast 4:22.4. This broke the previous race record—set, ironically by Fred Schoch's 1969 crew—for the Kent course by nearly ten seconds and was the fastest mile ever rowed by a Kent crew on its home course, whether in practice or in a race. (The books were closed on our record when the length of the racecourse changed to 1,500 meters the following year.)[*]

———

A crew race consists of four basic parts: the start; followed by a "high" ten (or fifteen, or twenty) fast strokes; the "settle"; and a closing sprint. In order to get a boat moving from a dead start, a crew takes several rapid short strokes using perhaps half or three-quarters the length of their slides. The oarsmen then lengthen their strokes to nearly full slides but still row at a fairly high rate for the next twenty strokes or so. The coxswain will then call on the crew to settle, which means to reduce the tempo. (The cadence for a start is usually in the neighborhood of forty-three to forty-five strokes per minute; the settle will take it down to the mid-thirties.) This is the pace at which most of the race will be rowed, though the cox may strategically call for a "power ten" in an attempt to make a move on a competitor. Finally, in the last 500 meters or so, the coxswain will call for a sprint, during which the cadence increases and, as one description aptly has it, the crew "pulls to exhaustion."

By the time of the Washington-Lee tilt, we had started to feel comfortable with the way Roger and Murray would

---

[*] This having been said, records can be meaningless in rowing, since conditions can vary widely from racecourse to racecourse and from season to season.

manage a race. A familiar pattern was established that made the "body" of the race our bread and butter; this is where our races would be won or lost. While a fast start is always desirable, settling down to a strong but moderate stroke count was where our oarsmanship really paid off. We made few mistakes, even in less than desirable conditions. Ever the onboard coach, Roger would tell us if one of us was "late" or "skying" our oars. There are many little things that can compromise the speed of a boat, so even the strongest oarsmen won't be successful if they can't keep their boats on an even keel by developing what is known as a good blade.

Our success to this point in the season was threatened shortly after the Washington-Lee race when Fred Elliott stood up in morning assembly to announce Murray's birthday on April 25, a declaration he soon came to regret. Because for years one's birthday at Kent was celebrated with the hazing ritual of being tossed into a nearby pond, following dinner that evening a mob descended on Murray and started to haul him away. There was little we could do to stop them. The pond, not yet fully replenished from spring runoff, might as well have been a pit. After swinging Murray back and forth for maximum effect, they let him fly. He ended up landing in shallow water square on his shoulder, sending him immediately to the infirmary. "Crew is down," Roger noted in his log for the day. Hart Perry was furious, sending the perpetrators of the stunt into dormitory exile for several days.

Throughout the week it was uncertain whether Murray would be available for our next race at Mount Hermon, on the Connecticut River in Massachusetts. We practiced throughout the week with Clint Whistler at stroke, moving Kershaw to the four seat and moving a man from the second boat to take over at two. Though Roger noted that "we moved very well in places" during our first practice without Murray, the next day he found the boat "very shaky." When we practiced at Mount Hermon on Friday, April 28, though, Murray was back at stroke, but still in some pain.

Mount Hermon was a rival you could despise for any number of reasons. First and foremost, its coach, Chuck Hamilton, was a Kent graduate who had long since renounced his allegiance to the school. He was also not what you'd call a model of good sportsmanship: For sleeping quarters at Mount Hermon, we were offered the cold, hard floor of the gymnasium. When Hamilton took Roger out to survey the course prior to the race, he pointed vaguely to an area of the river and said, "That's where you want to be." Skeptical, Roger picked up a piece of wood and tossed it where "we wanted to be." It promptly started swirling, indicating a speed-killing eddy. Finally, though Kent had beaten Mount Hermon in a match race the previous year, it had lost to the boat later in the spring at the New England championships in the most dismal of ways: The number two man had "caught a crab" in the final sprint, stopping the Kent boat dead in the water.*

---

* The Mount Hermon boat in 1971 was stroked by Al Shealy, perhaps the finest oarsman to come out of New England. More on him later.

Monotony, at times, can betray a welcome consistency. We jumped out to a length lead after just twenty-five strokes, then were assisted by turnabout when a Mount Herman oarsman suddenly caught a crab. With most of the race still to go Mount Hermon had plenty of time to catch up, but once we settled we continued to move out on them: At the half-mile point we were up by two lengths; we extended that to four lengths by the time we reached the finish line. Though it had been a relatively easy race, Murray and his shoulder had had enough. He and Roger switched positions for the row back to the dock, Murray the burly coxswain facing Roger the diminutive stroke.

Following the Mount Hermon race we went on hiatus for two weeks, at least as far as competition was concerned.* During this time Murray rested his shoulder for a few days, while the rest of us practiced in smaller boats and ran to maintain our conditioning. I rowed bow in a four with coxswain, while the others alternated between the four, a double scull, and a single scull. After three days in the four, Roger noted that "that 4+ is pretty good." When Murray returned on May 4 we had two practices, since the school was on a self-decreed holiday. Of the morning session Roger wrote, "Good practice [though] rusty—catches not sharp and completely together, finishes messy."

For the afternoon practice Hart Perry had decided it was time to give Pa Brown his crack at the first boat. Elliott

---

* We did race a crew composed of Kent alumni on Sunday, May 7, and beat them by two lengths. Half the crew was made up of oarsmen from 1971.

was moved to bow and Brown took over at the three seat. As expected, I was moved to seven on the second boat.

Why Hart Perry (whom by now we also affectionately referred to as the Boss) would tamper with the boat's chemistry at this point is a question I have long pondered, my wounded ego notwithstanding. Perhaps Perry was just trying to be fair to Brown, believing you shouldn't lose your chance to crack a starting lineup just because of an injury. Perhaps he wanted to see if the boat would really be faster than it already was. After asking several of Hart's oarsmen about his coaching style, the latter explanation seems to be the closest to the truth. Here we had a stretch of time where he could afford to innovate, and innovation was the hallmark of Hart Perry's coaching. He even second-guessed himself, bringing in other coaches to critique everything from our starts to our sprints. (Rusty Robertson, coach of a New Zealand crew that won an Olympic gold medal in 1968, was brought to Kent during the winter of 1971–72 to work on our stroke, emphasizing leg strength.) When Murray suggested that Hart tone down his emotional prerace talks so as not to push the already wound-up younger oarsmen over the edge, he took Murray's advice—most of the time.

Hart Perry was also something of a visionary when it came to equipment. Kent was one of the first schools, college or prep, to acquire an ergometer. Kent made the switch from oars with long and thin blades to "spoons," or more oval blades, well before many other crews had. And as demonstrated by the acquisition of the *Sill,* the boats themselves had to embody all of the latest innovations and designs. Indeed, the first boat was replaced about once every two years to stay up with the latest improvements. In terms of the quality and quantity of its equipment, the Kent boathouse was one of the finest in New England if not the country, which partially explains why the Olympic trials were held at Kent during the summer of 1972.*

So, in retrospect, I shouldn't have been surprised that Hart was going to give Brown a shot at the first boat at my expense. Leavening the drama was the fact that Pa Brown didn't much care for me. A proud Southerner, he may have viewed a seat on the first boat as his entitlement and me as some undeserving Yankee usurper. Before or after his tryout, I can't remember when, he even took great offense at something I said at dinner, reached across a table to grab me by the tie, and proceeded to scream at me. To this day I have no idea what that was all about; it may well have been born of frustration.

Pa Brown lasted with the first boat for all of two practices. Of the first practice the afternoon of May 4, Roger wrote: "Pa gets his shot. Bad practice. *Rushed.*" After practice on May 5, Roger noted that it "started well . . . [then] gradually fell apart." Moreover the port side was consistently outpulling starboard, and Brown was on the starboard side. If Roger didn't overcorrect the boat would end

---

* Because the Kent course was too narrow, the trials were actually rowed at nearby Lake Waramaug. I participated, but the only exercise I got was with my thumb as a timer for the heats.

up going in circles. Like a dog awaiting his master, that afternoon I stood atop a knoll waiting for the Boss and the first boat to dock. When Murray got out of the boat he looked for me, and when he found me he simply shook his head. Later Perry walked up to me and said, "You're back in tomorrow," emphasizing the point with a poke in the chest. In hindsight, if I had known about something else Roger wrote of the practices with Pa Brown, I may not have doubted myself so much: "No feeling of unity w/o Rinehart."

With that elephant out of the way, we could turn to the daunting challenges that remained: three regattas against substantially better competition.

VI

MEN OF KENT

"Champions aren't made in the gyms. Champions are made from something they have deep inside of them—a desire, a dream, a vision."

—Muhammad Ali

Befitting the times, the Kent student body in 1972 contained its fair share of what I would call fashionable rebels, or those who deigned to challenge conventional wisdom and authority simply because it was de rigueur to do so. And like patriotism in those days, school pride was not to be worn on one's sleeve. Emblematic of the American culture at large, Kent was divided into those who played by the rules and those who would like you to think that they didn't, but actually did. (Habitual offenders of the school's decorum seldom lasted long.) Subject to an environment of strict athletic discipline within a rigorous academic and social one, the oarsmen of the Kent School Boat Club clearly fell into the former category. But respect begot respect: We were treated like adults so long as we stayed in line. The irony of this, as shall be seen, is that we were allowed to do some very adult things away from campus that would never have been tolerated while on it.

Still, this is not to say that there wasn't a little pushback when it came to the politesse of the Kent School Boat

Club, which called for closely cropped hair and a generally clean look. Heavily bearded ones such as myself and
Charlie Poole dared the world with our below-the-lobe,
mutton-chop sideburns; Kershaw, Elliott, Rooney, and
Beach all wore signature hats that, as victory followed
victory, became sacred good luck charms. Elliott and Kershaw's topper of choice was a turned-down sailors' cap.
Murray wore a red beret that suggested "commando"
more than it did Parisian artiste.* John Rooney's look was
perhaps the oddest of all with his red-and-white ski cap,
whose tassel would bounce around with every stroke. So
if from the neck down we were a vision of uniformity,
eccentricity took over from the neck up. Hart Perry might
have protested, but his crew was winning, and he was not
about to deny anyone his talisman.

I had no such lucky charm but engaged in a prerace
ritual that accidentally became part of the warm-up routine
for the entire crew. Unable to settle my nerves before our
first race, I secluded myself in the corner of a field near the
boathouse and started jumping up and down as if I had
just discovered fire ants in my knickers. Thinking perhaps
that this was a new and exotic form of prerace preparation, Charlie Poole soon joined me and started doing the

---

* Murray was also known as "Sledge" for his square, sledgehammer-
like head. A small splitting maul usually traveled with us (but was
never carried on the boat) as his good luck charm. To demonstrate
how much things have changed over the last forty years, he had the
maul tucked into his belt when we went through JFK security on
the way to England. A security guard simply examined it and gave
it back to him.

same thing. Befitting the leader of some trendy cult, I came to lead the entire crew in this hysterical practice following our more traditional warm-ups before every race. Hart Perry must have rolled his eyes skyward at the scene of his crew bouncing around like so much exploding popcorn, but he didn't interfere. Like I said, we were winning.

The stylish aversion to cheerleading for the school meant that we had a rather small but loyal following. One who signed on early was John Menge, a fellow sixth former who took on the dirty work of managing the crew and attending to all the details that we would tend to overlook. Looking like he just walked off the set from an Andy Hardy movie, Bubbles (as he was known to us) cut an image of youthful gentility in his horn-rimmed glasses, bow tie, and oxford shirt. A gentlemanly Louisianan, Bubbles also had a twin identical by appearance only, and whose nickname, Rocky, clearly suggested something of a different attitude. Though sounding like exiles from some Saturday morning cartoon show, Bubbles and Rocky proved that individuality trumps genetics every time. Where John was happy to oversee the boathouse and help Roger with his pre- and postrace chores, Rocky was a physical type who occasionally rowed with the second boat. And because the boys were sorely missed by their mother, Sue, she had decamped from their home in New Orleans to rent a house in nearby Washington, Connecticut. In short order she had become not just John and Rocky's mother but everybody's mother *in loco parentis*. She was known to us, with palpable affection, as Sweet Sue.

Another fellow traveler from those days was Tully Vaughan, a member of the 1950 crew and the last Kent boat to win at Henley. Tully was no passive observer but a fill-in coach, occasional race umpire, van driver, and father-confessor to the crew. He also handled business details such as negotiating hotel room rates when we were traveling. The fact that he was a reminder of an embarrassingly long drought of Henley championships only served to motivate us further. If the crew had a guardian angel, it was Tully.

Of course parents and family were always around, and there was the seemingly unremitting ubiquity of Liz, but I've always singled out my precocious younger brother, Stephen, for his shameless moxie in reporting the crew's success to our hometown newspaper, the *Westport News*. Sounding part "Tick Tock" McGlaughlin from the movie *Seabiscuit* and part Red Barber, he once shamelessly boasted that because I rowed bow, "Rinehart is always the first one to cross the finish line." Since the articles were never bylined, the budding sports writer's objectivity could not be challenged.

Something, too, must be said of the shifting dynamic between me and Kent as I wound down my sixth form year. Except for some minor academic housekeeping, I already had one foot out the door, the other being firmly embedded in the hull of the *Frederick Herbert Sill*. Responsibilities eased as I prepared to turn my prefecture over to my logical successor, Charlie Poole. With parents ever available to take us where we wanted to in our free time, Liz and I spent as much time as we could away from campus. We had also made a commitment to the future and to each other by deciding to go to Kenyon College together in the fall.

The first of the three May regattas was our own, an invitational with Penn, Harvard, Syracuse, and Cornell freshman crews. We would row against heavyweight boats, whereas the second boat would take on lightweights. In the week leading up to the regatta, a number of us developed a bad case of nerves, and Roger even noted that we seemed scared for the first time all season. Liz found me at times completely unapproachable. The week had started out with some specialized coaching by Englishman John Dent, a former Andover coach who now lived in the Kent area. Dent emphasized power on the recovery, or just before the oar comes out of the water. According to Roger, we "flew on several pieces." But as the day of the regatta got closer our nerves had gotten the best of us, and we were "sluggish" at times. We had a bad practice on Friday—no swing—so whatever ailed us would have to be fixed as we warmed up for our first heat the following day.

Fortunately, we had time. The first two heats were raced by the lightweight boats with our Kent second beating Harvard, notwithstanding the fact that Kent rowed the last 200 meters with seven men. In rowing a mechanical mishap is a scourge if not necessarily commonplace, and in this instance the number four man had "jumped his slide," meaning he had pushed his seat off its track by not coming down on it squarely with his butt. Though this froze him in place for the rest of the race, the crew still managed to finish three seconds ahead of the Harvard boat.

The heavyweight crews all looked as though they outweighed us by at least forty pounds a man, and probably did. For our first race we drew Syracuse. Rowing in perhaps the best conditions so far that season—the sky was clear, the weather warm, and the river relatively flat—we got off to a good start and an even better settle in what was by now becoming a familiar pattern. By the quarter-mile mark we had a length lead, but Syracuse then had some mechanical issues of its own, recovered quickly, and challenged Kent for the lead. As Fred Elliott recalled, though, we "gave Syracuse nothing." Rowing at a moderate thirty-two strokes per minute, we finished five lengths ahead of the Orangemen. Except for perhaps the race with Yale at Derby, we had yet to have a close race that season.

That wouldn't change in the final. In the other opening heavyweight heat, Cornell had beaten Harvard handily and had posted a time that was actually four seconds faster than our 5:01 for the race with Syracuse. They also had, we were told, "an abundance of power" and were definitely "the crew to beat" in the regatta. In fact, after a fast start at a forty-four we found ourselves down by two seats. But we came back after the settle and took a three-quarter-length lead just before the quarter-mile marker. Roger then called for twenty leg drives to open up the lead further, and we were up by two lengths at the half. At the finish, the difference was three lengths. Rowing our best race so far that year, we had beaten a pretty good Cornell crew. Roger had one word for our performance: *beautiful.*

(Following us in a launch that contained Bubbles, Tully, Hart, and the race umpire, Tully heard "some jackass" behind him in the boat talking, a clear violation of rowing etiquette. He started to turn around to tell the guy to shut up when out of the corner of his eye he saw the Boss in the back saying, "Grind 'em! Grind 'em!" He left him alone.)

In addition to the ritual coxswain dunking, one of the traditional fruits of victory in a regatta is that you literally take the shirts off the backs of the vanquished (or more

Charlie Poole, the author, and Murray Beach after winning the Kent Regatta. Fred Elliott and Charlie Kershaw trail behind. *Author's Collection.*

politely, they have to give them to you). So it was that we earned some plunder from Harvard, Cornell, and Syracuse. "He's got his three shirts," Liz recorded for posterity in a scrapbook she gave me. "Now he's in a better mood. Now it's my turn."

Indeed it was. But Philadelphia, and a possible national championship, loomed.

Until the early 1820s, the Schuylkill River in Pennsylvania was a tidal stream that coursed wildly for 130 miles from its headwaters in the Appalachian Mountains before tumbling into a cataract (the Falls of the Schuylkill) at Philadelphia and ultimately feeding the Delaware River. In order to make the river navigable and provide water power for the city, a dam was completed in 1821 near what is now the Philadelphia Museum of Art. Named the Fairmount Dam, its construction intentionally led to the "ponding" of the river behind it, flooding over the cataract as well as several small islands. Above the dam the Schuylkill was now wide and flat and less susceptible to the unpredictability of a freshet. It quickly became a Mecca for the sport of rowing.

Rowing on the Schuylkill was forever immortalized in the art of the American realist Thomas Eakins, a sculler himself who from 1871 to 1874 produced dozens of paintings, watercolors, and drawings of his fellow oarsmen. Marrying anatomy to geometry, his preliminary perspective drawings contained grids so he could precisely capture "the exactness which such a mathematical and conceptual approach afforded," according to one critic. Always placing his subjects in the warm light of a late afternoon or evening, his oarsmen are either paddling lightly or even idle, faithfully portraying the contemplative solitude of the single or double sculler. Notwithstanding his tremendous body of work, his rowing pictures demonstrated "an intensity of focus that he would never repeat with any other subject."

Amid gambling scandals associated with professional rowing, the Schuylkill Navy of Philadelphia was formed in 1858 to promote amateurism on the river. The oldest amateur athletic governing body in the United States, the Schuylkill Navy comprises ten clubs on Philadelphia's famed Boathouse Row, including Vesper Boat Club, one of the most recognized rowing clubs in the United States. The Schuylkill Navy also oversees several regattas every year, among them the Dad Vail, the largest collegiate rowing competition in the United States, and the Stotesbury Cup, generally regarded to be the world's oldest and largest high school regatta. Established by financier Edward T. Stotesbury in 1927, the Stotesbury Cup in 1972 was considered to all effects to be the national championship, since no other comparable high school regatta existed at the time. Kent did not start participating in the regatta until 1969, with its best finish, fifth place, coming in 1970.

Before departing for Philadelphia late on Thursday, May 18, we went out on the river and practiced our starts, finishing up with a 500-meter piece that Roger described as "much too rushed, keel terrible, each side pulling the other at different times." Still, when informed by the Boss that we had rowed the piece in one minute and fifteen seconds, he was astonished. Even though it had been rowed downstream, it was still extremely fast.* We were ready for Stotesbury.

The regatta was a two-day affair with preliminary heats on Friday and finals on Saturday. Because all classes of boats were represented, it was very much a case of "hurry up and wait" as we tried to kill time before our first race, scheduled for 6:15 Friday evening. In the morning we went out for a paddle, which Roger described as "flat," and surveyed the course. Because the course took a slight bend to the right after the start, the stake boats† would be staggered. There were about fifteen boats competing in the first eights, meaning three preliminary heats out of which the top two crews in each would compete in the final.

If we were unusually apprehensive about the competition, it was probably because we were also somewhat out of

---

* Our upstream times in other practices tended to be around one minute and twenty something. By way of comparison the Olympic record for 2,000 meters, held by the 2004 U.S. men's eight, is 5:19:85, or an average of about 1:20 for every 500 meters.

† An anchored boat or platform at the starting line of a racecourse where the stern of a shell or scull is held until the starting gun.

our element, having left the comfort of New England for the mid-Atlantic to face a brace of crews from the likes of Virginia, Delaware, Maryland, New York, and Pennsylvania, several of which intended to lay equal claim to the title of national champion. Similarly, so little was known about us that we were not even among the small group of elite crews favored to win the eights. In fact, the choice of many to win was Liverpool High School in Syracuse, a true heavyweight crew that averaged an intimidating 193 pounds per man and which had even beaten Syracuse University's varsity heavyweight crew in a mile race.

By the afternoon the weather had deteriorated and rain threatened. In its first heat the Kent second boat came in a disappointing third, fierce tailwinds causing several oarsmen to lose control of their sweeps. While we waited uncomfortably in our vans, Roger checked equipment and repeatedly reviewed race strategy in his mind: "Head for the lane under the bridge, then head for the second from left white square on the bridge past the finish line, then after a half mile head for the big red and blue P on the bridge—way to the left of lane 6." (We were to be in lane 5.) At one point Hart walked up to Roger and spooked him further by saying, "Watch out for St. Andrews," the crew that had won the Stotesbury Cup the previous year. In addition to St. Andrews, there were three other crews in our heat whose names were as mysterious to us as the collision of consonants and vowels that constituted the name of the host river: Father Judge, Fort Hunt, and the favorite in the heat, T. C. Williams.[*]

At about six o'clock the first eights started taking to the river. Not only would we be in the last heat of the day, but we were to be the last boat to go out on the river, meaning there would be precious little time to warm up. In fact, we only had time to practice a start and take ten power strokes before we were called to our stake boat. Although we were last on the stake boat, the crew from Father Judge repeatedly fell off its own stake boat, and with the wind blowing hard it became increasingly difficult to keep the boat straight while waiting for Judge to get it together. As we were making some adjustments to get the boat pointed downriver again, the starter decided enough was enough and just started the race. We were off.

Probably because of the staggered start, there are different recollections of how the race evolved. Although Fred recalled that we jumped out on Williams by a few seats at the start, Roger had us even with the Titans, with Father Judge slightly behind. St. Andrews and Fort Hunt faded so quickly that Roger stopped looking for them. At about the quarter-

---

[*] Yes, the very same T. C. Williams whose integrated football team made history the previous autumn, and was immortalized in the film "*Remember the Titans*" starring Denzel Washington as coach Herman Boone. In fact, two of Boone's players—Dan Carl and Kirk Barker—rowed on the T. C. Williams eight at Stotesbury. Of the result, Barker was later to recall, " . . . We were very disappointed, as ours was as high a caliber a crew as had been assembled in the Alexandria school system in quite some time. Each of the oarsmen ended up competing at the Division I level. Two of our members competed in the '76 Olympics.' "

mile mark Roger told us that Williams was up on us by about a quarter length, but those on shore claimed it was anywhere from a half to full length. Roger called for drives, felt the boat surge and then momentarily lose some control. Geoff had missed the water on a stroke, and as they had later admitted, so had Bones and Rooney. Still, with a quarter mile to go, Roger was opposite the T. C. Williams stern deck. Williams then went to a sprint early while we stayed at a thirty-six, but we continued to move on them. When at last we went to our sprint, Williams faded; Roger had the number five man as we crossed the finish line. But because of the staggered nature of the course, we weren't at first sure if we had won. Charlie Poole yelled to the shore to try to get confirmation and received a thumbs-up in reply from John's father.

Our final—and the last race of the regatta—was set for 3:00 p.m. the next day. True to form, Liverpool had also won its heat, and no doubt looked upon us bewilderedly as a boat full of undersize irritants that had somehow snuck into the final. T. C. Williams was certainly looking for revenge after what we had done to them in the first heat. Indeed, many viewed the final as a duel between Liverpool and Williams, with a possible challenge from J. E. B. Stuart, another Virginia school. The remaining crews—St. Josephs, Bonner, and Kent—would be reduced to mere spectators. We were certainly not expected to repeat the performance of the previous day.

In fact, we exceeded it. Though Liverpool took an early lead—its weight might have given it an advantage in the still-windy conditions—we never let them get ahead of us by more than half a length, at times battling a persistent Williams boat for second. St. Joseph's, Bonner, and Stuart were all in close pursuit, giving lie to the notion that the final would separate the men from the boys. At the half-mile mark, Roger called for leg drives, and we were able to move out on Williams slightly and directly challenge Liverpool for the lead. With 500 meters to go it was still anybody's race, but Roger and Murray had a trick up their sleeves. After baiting the opposing crews into what they presumed to be our finishing sprint at thirty-nine strokes a minute, Roger called upon us to take the pace even higher as we approached the finish line. Both Williams and Liverpool failed to keep up, fell back by half a length, and ran out of gas. We crossed the line in 4:35.4, a time that turned out to be the fastest mile ever recorded on the Schuylkill. Williams finished second, the vaunted Liverpool crew third, followed by St. Joseph's, Bonner, and Stuart.

Roger's private journal entry (as opposed to his log) for May 20, which he must have written as soon as we docked and secured the boat, captured the immediacy of the race.

Ready all—Row! 3/4-1/2-3/4—lengthen—come on— 3-4-5 drive.

I looked over—6 boats all even—a million oarsmen—a sea of oarsmen all across for one goal. Should I settle, should I settle . . . here. Ready, row—bam!* Good we're moving we're moving come

---

* "Ready all, row!" is the traditional way an umpire starts a race. When Roger commanded "ready, row" during a race it was code for telling us to start taking power strokes.

on. A couple of boats had dropped back—we were ahead of T. C. on the start—good. Into the bridge 10 leg drives, leg drives, go-go-go. Out of the bridge— Liverpool 3–4 seats ahead—no one else—everyone else back. I never saw J. E. B., Bonner, St. Joes. Coming up on the canoe club—wait wait wait 10 now! Leg Drives. Someone remembered the coach on shore—"Take 10, take 10." I heard nothing. Ready row Murray [?] . . . yea ready row yea! Legs down I looked over—a line of boats straight across behind us. Liver a bit ahead. I had the stern deck. I had cox. Murray—"ten" 10 leg drives—leg drives now now now. I got cox. 750 m. to go. Come on. We are even w/ Liverpool. Come on! Ready row? Yes. Ready—row . . . smash it smash it hold it hold it hold it—500 meters to go go get 'em! 500. Under the wire. I had stroke—Liverpool starts taking stroke up. 10 leg drives under the wire. Sprint? Yea—T. C. Even w/ Liverpool. T. C. coming up. Take it up. 36 to 39 we're moving. I got stroke—I got 7 move! Take it up. Up to 42! We're moving drive it in 20 more! I got 5 I got 4—3 strokes after island. Come on! I heard and saw the shore. A million people screaming. Drive it in! Waynough! Murray collapses . . .

Much later, Murray, not one given to hyperbole, would say that in the final at Stotesbury we had rowed the "perfect" race.

Fred Elliot signaling our win at Stotesbury. *Courtesy of Fred Elliott*

The press positioned our unexpected victory as a David versus Goliath story; in fact the *Philadelphia Inquirer* reporter, Chip Babcock, hadn't even done any research on us prior to the final (otherwise he might have known something about Kent's rowing traditions). After the race he was asking questions like "Who are you guys?" and "Where did you come from?" His article the next day in the *Inquirer* was a bit over the top, saying that our "lightweight" crew had "made history" by breaking the Schuylkill record for the mile and beating "two of the best crews in the nation." Murray was quoted as saying, "We were apprehensive about this regatta because we knew what had happened before. This year we were undefeated against New England opposition, but that hasn't meant much in the past."

Hoisting the Stotesbury Cup in Philadelphia—a national championship. From left to right: Elliott, Kershaw, Beach, Poole, Rinehart, O'Keefe, Rooney, Stewart, Whistler, Tully Vaughan, and Hart Perry.
Courtesy of Fred Elliott

Alas, my memory of the elation we felt after being presented with the Stotesbury Cup has long faded, but a photograph taken of all of us at that euphoric moment has come to be the most iconic artifact of our championship season. Hanging today near the *Sill* in the Kent Rowing Center, the picture might be to Kent rowing what Joe Rosenthal's photo of the flag raising at Iwo Jima is to the Marines. Standing behind the *Sill,* Geoff is hoisting the Cup as a number of us strain to reach it. Charlie Poole has one hand on the trophy's base with his other hand extended as if to say, "How about this, folks!" Then there is Tully and the Boss off to the side, Tully trying to take the measure of the crew while Hart flashes a grin that says "At last."

As we prepared to leave our hotel to return to Kent, the first boat was summoned to Tully's room for a brief meeting. As if to add to the suspense about the reason for the sudden gathering, Tully made us wait outside his door until all nine of us were there.

Once assembled, he opened the door and stepped aside to reveal two bottles of champagne and nine glasses. Curiously, Kent School Dean of Boys William Hartwell Perry Jr. was nowhere to be found.

———

On the way back to Kent from Philadelphia, the crews rode in the vans, except for Murray and John Menge. They rode with the Boss in the truck that carried the *Sill* and our gear. Hart wanted to have a talk, and not just a postmortem on Stotesbury. He wanted to talk about Henley. While the conventional wisdom was that we had to win the New Englands at Worcester, Massachusetts, the following weekend to earn a trip back to the United Kingdom, as a practical matter a decision had to be made now. Henley was only five weeks away; housing and flights had to be arranged, entry fees had to be paid, and he had to figure out how to get the *Sill* over there, since we certainly weren't going to row a borrowed boat. Just as important, he had to plan a training regimen leading up to our departure, which meant arranging for room and board and seeing to it that we had some regular competition to keep us sharp. In the end, Murray and Hart decided to split the difference: We would go to Henley, but the crew wouldn't be told until after Worcester. Bubbles, Murray, Hart, and certainly Sidney Towle would have to sit on this news for a week.

Hart may have been thinking ahead to England when he had us practice with a solid heavyweight crew from Marist College on Lake Waramaug in the week leading up to Worcester. On Wednesday, May 24, we rowed against them in three set pieces, two 500-meter sets with a 1,000-meter piece between. The first 500 was "rocky" and we never shook the Marist boat, ending up dead even with it. The 1,000 was "a little messy" but better, and we beat Marist by a length. In the last 500—"improving all the way"—we beat them by three-quarters of a length. Of practice, the next day Roger wrote, "We're much more at home. Smooth. A couple of pieces felt like a thirty-four but were at thirty-eight."

Our final regatta that spring took place on Saturday, May 27, on Lake Quinsigamond in Worcester, Massachusetts, and we could be forgiven if we viewed it as the least competitive of our three spring regattas. Founded in 1947, the New England Interscholastic Rowing Association's annual regatta began as a small affair with a handful of area crews but by 1972 had grown into an event involving dozens of boats in all classes. Arguably a lesser competition than Stotesbury, the New England regatta that year did present its challenges for us, such as a fast Exeter crew about which we knew little. The rest of the competition was fairly familiar; we had already beaten two of the crews, Mount Hermon and Andover, in match races earlier in the spring. And pride was at stake as well: On the occasion of the fiftieth anniversary of Kent School in 1956, Father Sill's sister had donated two trophies, for the champion eight and champion four, named for Kent's founder. Not winning the Sill Cup in any year would be not just embarrassing but shameful.

Anticipating a certain if not easy victory, our entourage to Worcester, Massachusetts, rivaled that of a touring rock band. In addition to the usual following of friends and parents, Father Pete Woodward and his wife came along, as well as several alumni, Sweet Sue, and of course Liz and her crowd. Photographs from that day recall that the mood was festive and celebratory even before we got out on the water, our crowd spread out on the banks of Lake Quinsigamond in a pageant of colorful blankets and coolers. Beer and champagne poured as freely as the warm light of a beautiful spring day. Such gaiety must have abetted my state of mind, for it was the first time that I felt absolutely positive that we would sweep an event. Stotesbury had been the crucible; Worces-

Tully Vaughan and Liz Pegram going over the race schedule for the New Englands at Worcester, Massachusetts. *Author's Collection.*

ter was just a matter of going out there doing what we were expected to do. Besides, Kent practically owned the place, having won five times in the previous ten years.

One who was not in a celebratory mood was Hart Perry, who paced the shoreline nervously smoking and with a look of foreboding on his face. Perhaps it's the races that you're supposed to win that a coach fears the most, but I think the Boss had more on his mind than that. This was his fastest crew in eleven years of coaching at Kent and, as it turned out, the high-water mark in a spectacular coaching career. He intuitively knew that he could take this crew to Henley and make a serious run at the Princess Elizabeth Cup, but a stumble at Worcester and the dream of an undefeated season would die hard. In the back of his mind he must have known that this crew could be his one shot at winning it all.

Hart Perry, looking for us at Worcester. *Author's Collection.*

His fears might have eased after the first heats. Keeping our stroke count low to conserve our energy for the final, we powered through a field that included Andover, St. Paul's, and St. John's, ultimately cruising to a four-second victory. Exeter won its heat as well, but by a slimmer margin, and their time over the course was no match for what we had done at a relatively sedate twenty-nine strokes per minute. Prior to the heat we had also noticed that the Exeter crew was somewhat cocky and undisciplined. Pulling up beside us, a few of their oarsmen engaged in some mild taunting. As always, we kept our heads forward and didn't respond. "Not an eye out of the boat—great!" Roger recalled.

"We have 'em right where we want 'em," Hart quipped.

As we approached the start for the final that afternoon, I kept telling myself, "Just one more time, one more time." The improbability of it all was as mysterious as ever, and as such made the moment wonderfully satisfying. My mother nailing a coin to a mast four years earlier and saying in effect, "Earn this." Eighteen years with nothing much to show for them athletically, until now. Not just a good crew, but a great crew. Undefeated, course records, a national championship, and a pretty girl to greet you when you came off the water. I thought of prayers during Adoration. Petals of faith. I thanked God for giving me this moment, and then paddled with eight of the finest men I had known to our stake boat.

We got off to a bad start. Distracted—perhaps looking ahead—our normal composure eluded us in the first strokes, and Exeter leaped out to a lead of nearly a length. Roger reported problems steering. Still, there was no panic. Roger settled us down and had Murray set the pace at thirty-five strokes per minute. When we started to pick up a seat or two on Exeter, I knew we had broken them. Roger said that he started to see "lots of eyes out of the boat" on the Exeter crew. At 750 meters Roger called for power and we further closed the gap; with 250 meters to go we had fully caught up to them. Our confidence restored, we proceeded to row right through Exeter as if they had decided to ship their oars and call it a day. Atoning for our poor start, perhaps, we were now rowing with as much skill, precision, and strength as we had at any time that spring. By the time we crossed the finish line in a record-setting 4:39.1, we were more than a length ahead of Exeter, the other crews so far behind that they looked as though they were in a different race altogether. I was so exhilarated that I felt as if I could row to England if I had to.

Tully had offered a nuanced account of the race as he and the Boss watched from near the finish. Actually, Hart refused to watch the start and handed his binoculars over to Tully. From there, Tully recalled the conversation going something like this:

Hart: "I think I'm going to be sick."

Tully: "Just do it to windward."

Tully: "We're off."

Hart: "How are we doing?" [We were down a length at this point.]

Tully: "We're hangin' in there."

Hart: "How are we doing?" [Still behind but now moving on Exeter.]

Tully: "We're right in there."

Hart then turned around to watch the last two minutes of the race. If he had seen the start, he might have died a small death then and there. Instead, as John Elliott later recalled, the Boss had a rum and coke for "each and every one of us" back at our motel later that evening.

───────

On Thursday, June 1, Roger, Murray, Geoff, Fred, Bubbles, Rocky, and Liz and I all graduated. Prior to the ceremony we had a morning practice. Roger noted:

Went out for a Prize Day row.

Really flying.

The No. 1 crew in the nation:

Bow: Rick Rinehart
2 Charlie Kershaw
3 Fred Elliott
4 John Rooney
5 Geoff O'Keefe
6 Clint Whistler
7 Charlie Poole

Stroke: Murray Beach
Cox: Roger Stewart

———

Following a long weekend break we returned to an empty Kent campus on Monday, June 5, to start preparing for Henley. In the meantime Sid Towle had sent out a letter to our parents requesting permission for us to travel to England. Towle's tone was businesslike and to the point:

> *The year 1972 marks the fiftieth year of rowing at Kent and one of the finest crews in the history of the school. Kent rightfully can be considered the top school crew in the United States having conquered all its opponents. . . .*
>
> *Consequently, we plan to send the crew to England to continue Kent's tradition of competing in the Henley Royal Regatta. We will compete at Henley only to minimize expenses and to concentrate fully on bringing back the Princess Elizabeth Cup.*
>
> *Will you, therefore, kindly advise me by return mail whether you are willing to have your son . . . join in the trip to England and to what extent you will participate in the defrayment of the costs. In this respect it also in the Kent tradition that those who are able to do so assist with the expenses of*

*another and such generosity would, of course, be
most helpful and appreciated.*

The other issue to be dealt with was getting the *Sill*
safely to England. For transport on land the boat could be
taken apart amidships so that the two sections, bow four
and stern four, could rest side by side on the outsize rack
of a pickup truck. But this wouldn't do for the cargo hold
of a Boeing 707. Not only was the boat awkward to handle
by even the most careful ground crews, the possibilities for
damage while in flight were just too great to chance. The
boat sections would have to be crated, and not just in any
old crates, but ones that would have to anticipate the mis-
calculations of a forklift driver.* One blemish in the *Sill*'s
tender skin would render the boat worthless to us. It was
decided that the only remedy was to have Helmut Schoenbrod custom-build the crates, an expense the school could
not afford. Fortunately, a number of the parents rose to the
occasion and agreed to pick up the cost.

And yet another precaution had to be taken: We needed
to bring along a spare oarsman as insurance against one of
us getting sick or injured. While there were several fine oarsmen on the second boat, Murray and Hart decided that its
stroke, Garth Griffin, would provide the best combination
of oarsmanship and companionability. (He had also been
voted commodore of Kent School Boat Club for 1972.) And

---

* Sure enough, when the *Sill* was delivered to us at Henley, one of
  the crates had the telltale signs of forklift blades stabbing its flank.

since we weren't bringing along John Menge, Garth could serve as manager as well. If we ever had to use Garth in the boat, however, his presence there would certainly challenge our "lightweight" reputation, especially if he took over for Bones or Kershaw. He weighed nearly 200 pounds.

Our practices the first day back from graduation were clearly aimed at getting us prepared for Henley's arduous one-mile, 555-yard course. At 2,112 meters it was not only longer than any course we had raced on that spring, but it was also upstream, which meant we'd be rowing against the current. An average time over the course for a decent eight rowing in relatively normal conditions would be about seven to seven and a half minutes, or about 50 percent longer than we had been accustomed to. So it was no surprise that Hart started working on our endurance first thing. In the morning we each put in three minutes on the ergometer, then went out in small boats to shake off the rust from being away for three days. The evening presented the day's biggest test with a row from the dam near Bulls Bridge to the boathouse—four miles—at full power. The stroke count was low, however, averaging about a twenty-seven, with intermittent sets at thirty-four and a final sprint at forty-two. "Tough!" Roger noted, but "better than even spacing all the way." Roger also figured that we had taken more than 750 power strokes that evening.

The long row was followed by relatively mediocre practices over the next several days, although our expectations for ourselves were much higher than they had been three months earlier. If we couldn't find our swing immediately, it was a bad practice. We also no longer had the second boat to row against, or any competition for that matter, so on Thursday, June 8, we decamped for one of America's most celebrated boathouses, the Harvard facility on the Thames River* near Groton known as Red Top, to tug on Superman's cape a bit.

The Harvard rowing program has been consistently as good as any college or university (or even Olympic) athletic program in America for nearly two centuries. Although we had technically "beaten" the Harvard second freshmen heavies by prior elimination at the Kent Regatta, the first freshman heavies were something to behold, quite possibly the best crew, period, in the United States in 1972. The talent started at stroke with Al Shealy, who would go on to stroke the U.S. national eight from 1973 to 1976, win a world championship in 1974, and later be inducted into the Rowing Hall of Fame in Mystic, Connecticut. The boat also included a fine oarsman from Kent's 1971 boat, Ed Woodhouse, probably the biggest, strongest, and most competitive oarsman to come out of an otherwise hapless crew that year. Right behind Woodhouse at the number six seat was Tiff "the Hammer" Wood, who would later represent the United States in three Olympics. The undefeated Harvard crew was preparing not only for their annual four-mile race with Yale, but for Henley as well, in their particular

---

* Pronounced *Thaymes*, with a soft "Th," by denizens of the Nutmeg State.

case a run at the Thames Challenge Cup. Over the next two days we would go at each other in short pieces with mixed results, but giving both crews something to brag about.

Red Top and its Yale counterpart at Gales Ferry are the crews' homes away from home and exist solely for housing oarsmen and equipment for the schools' nearly 160-year-old annual duel. The first race was held in 1852, making it America's oldest intercollegiate athletic competition and predating the Harvard-Yale football rivalry by more than two decades. Although Yale was the first of the two schools to introduce rowing, Harvard has dominated the event, winning 90 of 134 races in the varsity eights alone through 2009. The race has been held annually since 1859, and has only been suspended for both of the twentieth-century's world wars.

Practicing alongside us and the first freshman heavies was another Harvard boat containing a collection of stray Harvard heavyweight oarsmen looking for a little competition. No match for either Kent or their Harvard brethren, they consistently fell behind in all of our set pieces, leaving the crews of Beach and Shealy to go at each other with all the urgency of a long-standing rivalry. (Murray, Shealy, Woodhouse, and Wood had been rowing with and against each other for a few years, so the competitive impulse was real.)

Our first outing with Harvard on the evening of June 8 did not go well. In fact, Roger recorded that on each of twelve sets of thirty-stroke pieces, "We got our clocks cleaned."

Practice the next morning was much better; we stayed with Harvard all the way. Roger attributed the improvement to better composure—"cool, calm, and collected." Part of the reason for our poor practice the previous evening may have been that the Thames at Groton is a rather intimidating body of water. Though not very long, the river is up to a mile wide in some places, and in the evening mist one could easily conjure a sense of being adrift at sea. And with its sprawling sub base, Groton evoked the eerie specter of nuclear annihilation, a prospect that still gave one jitters in 1972. In fact, when we were resting briefly between sets during the morning practice, I glanced over my shoulder only to see a menacing-looking black submarine emerge from the fog and approach our port side. *I don't want any of that,* I thought to myself. Fortunately the sub was moving slowly and we could comfortably ride out the roll from its wake.

We returned to Kent for two more days of practices on June 10 and 11, our last practices in the United States. The final practice on Sunday morning was a Henley-like seven-minute row at full power, which Roger thought "felt very good." In the afternoon we crated the *Sill* and our other gear and started packing for England.

Our flight departed on Monday, June 12, at 9:15 a.m. from JFK in New York. A number of things about that flight and flying decorum and safety in 1972 will give seasoned twenty-first-century travelers pause. First of all, the departure time: Before the hub and spoke system of air travel was developed following deregulation in 1978, there was no compelling financial need to have a domestic flight meet an international flight to transfer passengers. (Thus the preference today for overnight flights to Europe to give travelers most of the day to get to their pertinent departure hub.) Prior to deregulation, profits were virtually guaranteed by the federal government, leading to such inefficiencies in the system. Furthermore, security was not intended to prevent terrorists from flying planes into buildings, but rather to prevent Cuban émigrés from hijacking planes and commanding them to Havana.* In mid-1972 crude metal detectors started appearing at major airports like JFK, but since, as I recall, we were allowed to each carry along two quart cans of Hawaiian Punch to avoid dehydration in the rarefied air, security did not anticipate the possibility of a loaded can of fruit juice being hurtled down the aisle of an airliner by a highly conditioned athlete. Finally, economy class in those days offered all the perquisites of today's first class: leg room, a hot meal served on bone china, and an open bar (which, of course, we could not take advantage of). Perhaps this is why people in 1972 tended to dress up for a flight; we all wore jackets, ties, and slacks (as opposed to jeans) not so much because we were representing Kent School, but rather because it was the thing to do then.

---

* Why anyone would want to hijack a plane to an impoverished, oppressive third-world nation from the United States is something that I've had a difficult time explaining to my children. The rash of hijackers from 1960 to about 1980 appear to have been a mixed bag of extortionists, the mentally ill, and Cubans looking to circumvent the U.S. embargo on flights to Cuba following the rise of Fidel Castro. By the early 1970s both governments had seen enough and agreed to cooperate in the prosecution of hijackers.

A little after 10 p.m. that night we arrived in London to a virtually empty Heathrow Airport. (Once again present-day travelers will find this hard to believe, for if there is one word to describe Heathrow nowadays, it's *bustle,* 24-7.) Like security procedures at JFK, customs was if not lackadaisical then certainly giving us the benefit of any doubt. Showing affinity for a recent wartime ally, but with a caveat, a Cockney customs inspector in the manner of Stanley Holloway stamped my passport while hardly looking at it. "Good luck boys," he told us. "But I hope you lose." His sense of national pride crystallized a notion that had been building in us since the New Englands at Worcester, that once abroad we were no longer competing just for ourselves, but now for our country as well.

In fact, our congressman, Stewart McKinney—a Kent graduate—had already suggested to President Nixon that he start reading deep into the sports pages toward the end of June to follow the Kent crew as well as that of another son of Connecticut, Al Shealy. (We did indeed receive a letter of congratulations from the president upon our return to the United States.) The president may have viewed this as a welcome distraction, since less than a week after our arrival in England, five men had been arrested after being caught breaking into Democratic National Committee headquarters in the Washington, D.C., office complex known as Watergate, catalyzing a series of events that would lead to Richard M. Nixon's resignation a little over two years later.

VII

TEMPLE ISLAND TO HOME

"Earthly glory is transitory, but there is always Henley."

—BENJAMIN IVRY, *REGATTA*

Our home for the next three weeks was to be the imposing residence of Commander Eric Gibson and family in Wargrave, Berkshire (or just Berks) County, about five miles from Henley. We arrived at the Gibsons' just after midnight on Tuesday, June 13, and got what sleep we could. Anxious to see the place that had only existed in our dreams up until now, those of us who were first-timers at Henley probably slept the least well. The majesty of the setting with its magnificent grandstand and seemingly endless series of white tents and blue-striped tents by the river was finally revealed to us when we were taken to the course at about ten in the morning. Because the *Sill* would not be delivered until later in the evening, we ran the towpath that parallels the course up to its start at Temple Island and back again, a distance of about four miles. When the *Sill* arrived at 8:30 that evening, we quickly put it together and were on the water by 9:00 p.m. We took a light paddle up to Fawley, the name for the halfway point on the course, but soon the long evening of a northern latitude summer began to dissolve into night. We returned to our dock and secured the *Sill* in Henley Royal Regatta Boat Tent Number One adjacent to the Leander Club, the traditional home for the Kent School Boat Club in England.

———

Henley is a Saxon name meaning "high enclosure" or "clearing." The town has represented an important crossing of the Thames since Roman times, its present bridge having been completed in 1774. Known throughout its early history as a popular coaching town, meaning a place where a coach and its passengers could stop for a cup of mead at the Catherine Wheel or a bed at the Red Lion Inn, it was especially favored by the likes of Dr. Johnson, Boswell, and Charles I. It was also home to England's only elected Pope, Nicholas Brakspear, elevated to the title of Pope Adrian IV in 1154. As previously mentioned, the first sanctioned crew race on the Thames at Henley occurred in 1829 when Oxford defeated Cambridge in eight-oared "cutters" before some 20,000 spectators.

Henley's long reach[*] was becoming so popular with oarsmen by the late 1830s that the town fathers thought that something formal should be done about it. On March 26, 1839, a Captain Edmund Gardiner suggested:

———

[*] Literally meaning "stretch of river between bends."

*that from the lively interest which had been mani-
fested at the various boat races which have taken
place on the Henley reach during the last few years,
and the great influx of visitors on such occasions,
this meeting is of the opinion that the establishing
of an annual regatta, under judicious and respectable management, would not only be productive of
the most beneficial results to the town of Henley,
but from its peculiar attractions would also be a
source of amusement and gratification to the neigh-
bourhood, and the public in general.*

"Originally staged by the Mayor and people of Henley as a public attraction with a fair and other amusements," the official history of the regatta reads, "the emphasis rapidly changed so that competitive amateur rowing became its main purpose." The first regatta was held in the summer of 1839 and took place on a single afternoon. By the next year it was up to two days, by 1866 it was at three days, and by 1906, four. The regatta received royal patronage from Prince Albert in 1851, an honor that has been renewed by each monarch since.

Since there were few sporting organizations in the world in the mid-nineteenth century on which to model the regatta, Henley organizers, later known as the Stewards, more or less had to make it up as they went along. However, so efficient became the management of the regatta by the turn of the twentieth century that the founder of the modern Olympics, Pierre de Coubertain, adopted some of the principles of Henley's "Stewardship" in forming the first International Olympic Committee. And though the regatta plays by its own rules and traditions, it is nevertheless recognized by the governing body of rowing in England and Wales, the Amateur Rowing Association, and, more important, by FISA,[*] the International Federation of Rowing Associations.

At the first Henley Regatta in 1839 (it was not yet "Royal") only one trophy was offered, the Grand Challenge Cup, "to be rowed for annually by amateur crews in eight-oared boats." The first competition for four-oared boats with coxswain came along in 1841with the establishment of the Stewards' Challenge Cup, which amusingly begat a coxswainless four contest in 1869 as a response to an incident that had occurred the previous year. Evidently, according to the official Henley history, at the 1868 regatta oarsman W. B. "Guts" Woodgate on a Brasenose four had found his coxswain an "encumbrance" and had ordered him to jump out of the boat at the start. (Woodgate had figured out how to work a steering mechanism using his foot.) "Lightened by the ejection of this passenger," the citation goes on to explain, "the Brasenose four went on to win easily—only to be disqualified." The Stewards' Challenge Cup itself went officially coxless in 1873, and over the following decades trophies were added for sculls, double sculls, pairs, and several new classifications for eights. By 1972 the Henley Royal Regatta offered twelve separate competitions.

---

[*] Fédération Internationale des Sociétés d'Aviron

Columbia University provided the first American crew to win at Henley, capturing the Visitors Challenge Cup for coxless fours in 1878, but it wasn't until 1914 that a crew from the United States, a Harvard boat, won the Grand Challenge Cup. It was also just the third foreign crew to do so in seventy-five years of competition for the Grand. Indeed, the Grand, and Henley as a whole, was dominated by English crews until competition was resumed following V-E Day in 1945. This had more to do with the paucity of foreign entrants (Kent and a few others excepted) than the inability of the rest of the world to produce worthy crews.[*] The international diversity of entrants increased markedly following the war, with crews from Europe, the Soviet Union, Germany, and Australia joining the United States on the engraving plate of Henley trophies. In Olympic years the regatta came to be viewed as a warm-up for the Games held later that summer.

One American Olympian who never had the chance to "warm up" at Henley was John B. "Jack" Kelly, perhaps the greatest sculler the United States has produced, and whose controversial exclusion from the regatta in 1920 may have single-handedly led to the Stewards' reconsideration of what an amateur was a decade and a half later. Born to Irish immigrant parents in Philadelphia in 1889, Kelly's was the archetypical American success story. A high school

---

[*] For example, in the sixteen Olympics from the debut of the modern games in 1900 until 1972, the United States won gold in the eights eleven times. Interestingly, for the London Olympics of 1908 and 1948, the rowing competition was held on the Henley course.

dropout, Kelly went to work for his brother's construction company in 1907, where he learned the bricklayer's trade. About two years later he started rowing out of the Vesper Boat Club boathouse on the Schuylkill; by 1916 he was the best sculler in the United States and a national champion. Upon his return from service in World War I in 1918, he started his own bricklaying company, and such was his talent for self-promotion that his business venture eventually made him a millionaire.

By the time of his application to compete in Henley's Diamond Sculls, Kelly had won six national championships and was in the midst of an incredible 126-race winning streak. Assured by the secretary of the National Association of Amateur Oarsman (NAAO), who had supposedly cleared Kelly's application in advance with the Stewards, Kelly bought himself a brand-new scull and made arrangements for passage to England. On the eve of his departure, he was shocked to receive a telegram from the Stewards that read simply: ENTRY REJECTED. LETTER FOLLOWS. As enraged as an Irishman could be after yet another seemingly typical slight by the English, Kelly took his revenge by beating the Henley sculls winner, Jack Beresford, at the 1920 Olympics.

As Kelly was one of the most famous athletes of his time, the Stewards' rebuff quickly became the stuff of populist outrage based on the wobbly conviction that his application was rejected solely because he had been "by trade or employment for wages a mechanic, artisan, or labourer." For Americans, whose passion for the little guy in such mismatches symbolized the struggle between commoner and nobility, even democracy against monarchy, this became the main story line. Facts are stubborn things, as the saying goes. The principal reason for the Stewards' rejection of Kelly's application was that they had essentially banned anyone from Vesper Boat Club from competing at the regatta after the club had publicly raised funds to send an eight over to Henley in 1905 to challenge for the Grand. This was viewed as payment to the Vesper crew, ergo professionalism. Only secondarily did the Stewards determine that "Mr Kelly was also not qualified under Rule I (e) of the General Rules (manual labour)." Still, the Kelly scandal embarrassed the Stewards into lifting the ban on Vesper entries shortly thereafter, and in 1937 all language denying applications to those who had been engaged in manual labor was expunged from the rules.

The story could have ended there, but Kelly chose to make his grudge against the Stewards multigenerational. As Benjamin Ivry recounts in his book *Regatta,* when John B. "Kell" Kelly Jr. was born, "His father vowed immediately that young Kell would vindicate the Henley Stewards' rejection by triumphing where his father had been excluded." Kell did so by winning the Diamond Sculls in 1949. Kelly Jr. also won the U.S. single sculls championship eight times and was a bronze medalist at the 1956 Olympics.

But Jack Kelly's sweetest revenge at the Stewards may have come after his death through his actress-daughter

Grace, later better known as Princess Grace of Monaco. Not only was she invited to present the trophies at the 1981 regatta, but in 2003 a women's quadruple scull competition at Henley was renamed the Princess Grace Challenge Cup. With that, it can safely be said, the Stewards had atoned for their indelicate snub of one of America's greatest athletes.

———

Over its long history two distinct but comingling Henleys have evolved, one the Henley of competition on the water, the other the social pageant under way on the banks of the Thames. A *Times* of London correspondent once referred to the latter as "one week when you drift back to the Edwardian era . . . in spite of the advanced technology of the sport on display." Venues for viewing racing are hierarchical, from the exclusive Stewards' Enclosure at the finish line, to the slightly more casual Remenham Club farther up the course, to the anything-goes decorum of simply plopping oneself down in the grass outside the enclosures and popping a bottle of champagne. The 1972 guide to the regatta tried to dispel "the mistaken impression . . . that admission to the enclosures was confined to those who . . . had something to do with rowing." "All are welcome," it stated with an air of generosity that came to a screeching halt with the caveat, "except for the Stewards' enclosure." Mere mortals were welcome to pay admission to something called the Regatta Enclosure, which provided "an excellent view of the racing . . . licensed bars and also amusement-with-prize machines." Sounding as if it was doing the general public a favor, the brochure concluded by saying that the Regatta Enclosure had a car park "which actually adjoins it."

Outside the Stewards' Enclosure at Henley. *Courtesy of Fred Elliott*

Because as a competitor my family was entitled to admission to the Stewards' Enclosure, the prospect of a trip to Henley had my mother and Liz scrambling to the dress shop and my father reviewing his fine wardrobe with particular gusto. A Web site known as the Twickenham Underground and its mysterious proprietor, "Rabbit," offers an irreverent but still helpful guide to dress code at Henley:

In brief the rules are fairly simple:

- *Lounge Suits or Blazers and Flannels for the gentlemen (and yes a shirt and tie is also a pre-requisite for admission)*
- *Skirts or dresses down to the knee for the ladies— no trousers divided skirts or culottes. (Well the rules were first designed in the eighteen forties.)—nb Remenham club doesn't require skirts to be below the knee, but you never know when you might be offered Stewards tickets, so better safe than sorry . . .*

The Stewards' own description of its Enclosure's dress code humorlessly affirms what Mr. or Ms. Rabbit suggests here, but ends with the rather severe "Mobile Telephones are forbidden"—not simply "not allowed" but "forbidden," as if they were the invention of the devil. As Benjamin Ivry deliciously describes in *Regatta,* such transgressions of Henley correctness are often met with the words "Not at Henley, please."

Still, in presenting the trophies at the 1949 regatta, Mrs. Winston (Lady) Churchill described Henley as "This lovely pageant of English life." In between races in 1972 spectators were entertained by the Band of the Irish Guards, whose program included such disparate melodies as "Gigi," "Swan Lake," and "Mary Poppins." Following the last race of the day, the band would play a somber "God Save the Queen," for which Britons and visitors alike would immediately cease conversation and freeze in place for the duration of the anthem. It was a reminder, if anyone needed reminding, that they were indeed in England, and that no other nation's flag would be flown nor its anthem played during the regatta, even at the presentation of trophies. Not at Henley, please.

Henley is and always has been a bacchanalia of food and drink. What beer is to NASCAR, Pimm's Cup and champagne are to Henley. For the uninitiated, Pimm's Cup, particularly Pimm's Cup Number 1, is derived from gin though it has amber coloring and hints of citrus and spice. "The traditional choice," according to Rabbit's rules of Henley etiquette, is "one part Pimm's, three parts lemonade, drunk in

A typical Henley picnic. *Courtesy of Fred Elliott*

pints. And since a healthy diet contains five portions of fruit or veg daily," Rabbit further recommends "a minimum of five pints of Pimm's per day." Pimm's can also be mixed with champagne or sparkling wine to create what is known as Royal Pimm's Cup. Accompanied by a full-blown, five-course meal or just a basket of strawberries, Pimm's and champagne are staples of the Henley picnic.

By 1972 Kent had been competing at Henley for nearly half a century and could claim a little Henley lore of its own, several incidences having to do with breaches of the regatta's singular decorum. It started rather ignominiously with Kent's first Henley visit in 1927 when Father Sill scandalously coached from a launch, evidently "forbidden" by the Stewards. (One presumes that coaching was to be done from the towpath, either on bicycle or on foot.) As recounted by Christopher Dodd in his history of the Regatta, "Nobody spoke to the boys from Kent for five days." However, Dodd explains, they nevertheless had "a warm reception at Mr. John Nugee's house at Radley," out of which contact "grew the annual exchange scheme run by the English Speaking Union," another dream of Father Sill's from that rainy day at Henley six years earlier.

A Kent crew was also famously responsible for some property damage to a Henley landmark in 1947. Following its victory over Tabor for the Thames Challenge Cup, John Elliott (who accompanied but did not row with the crew) recalled a celebration that took place at the Red Lion Inn in Henley:

We ended up out on the upstairs porch of the hotel, a bunch of us, feeling no pain. We were laughing, carrying on, jumping up and down and all of a sudden the floor gave way and the porch collapsed one story to the ground. Fortunately no one was seriously hurt.

Amazingly, the innkeeper was nothing but apologetic and doted on the boys and their minor injuries. He took the blame for having built a flimsy porch, ignoring the fact that the boys' continual stomping probably led to its collapse. As Elliott concluded, "Those British! They are the nicest people."

The 1950 crew was in a rivalry with the Yale varsity lightweights that was so intense that good sportsmanship had to be eschewed to silence outright contempt, even at the manners-conscious Henley Royal Regatta. Kent had beaten Yale by three-quarters of a length earlier in April at Derby, notwithstanding the fact that the Kent bowman had caught a crab close to the finish. Both crews went on to win the rest of their races in the U.S., the Yale crew said to be "the best light crew in twenty-three years," and both aimed to capture the Thames Challenge Cup at Henley. The Kent crew at first took a magnanimous view, but soon found that "the usual camaraderie between Americans while abroad did not exist." As Kent's number two man, Jim Young, recalled, "at Henley the Yalies wouldn't even talk to us. If we approached them on the street, they crossed it. Obviously, they were told and agreed to have no contact with us." Moreover, Yale was favored to win the Thames by the London press, "so why this fear of a small New England prep school?"

As it happened, Kent met Yale in the quarterfinal for the Thames, jumped out to a comfortable lead, and by the halfway point at Fawley, Yale was well behind the Kent boat. Here, the ever-scrupulous Tote Walker—an adherent to the English tradition of winning "modestly" if there ever was one—might have signaled for the Kent boat to gain no more open water on Yale. (Kent had already reduced its stroke to a twenty-three to keep the Yale boat no more than two lengths behind.) Instead, Walker turned his back on the race, effectively leaving the choice of how to finish up to the crew. Young recalled "that it didn't take us long to agree that this situation did not call for good sportsmanship. We all agreed to let it rip." Kent edged up to a forty-four, and put another length between themselves and Yale at the finish. Fairly or not, a headline in a London paper the next day openly seethed: KENT INSULTS YALE.

Twenty-two years later the number five man on the 1950 crew, Tully Vaughan, threatened to add another anecdote to the narrative of Kent crews at Henley when he made this challenge to us: "If you win the Princess Elizabeth Cup," he teased, "I will jump into the Thames fully clothed."

The format for the Henley Royal Regatta is unique in the world of rowing in that the narrow course allows for only two lanes, meaning that its organization is more like that of a tennis tournament rather than a traditional multilane regatta with its qualifying heats and redeeming repechages.* Winners are determined on a knockout basis, meaning that once you've lost, you're a mere spectator for the rest of the regatta. The two-lane format also has a social element to it, however, since the breadth of the river has actually accommodated three lanes, though over a shorter course, for such events as the 1948 London Olympics. Protected by a continuous line of booms consisting of sixty-foot sections of timber, the course allows for spectators to view racing from pleasure boats outside the booms. The booms not only delineate a boundary but also help ensure calm water conditions on the course. The cavalcade of diverse pleasure craft is a spectacle in itself and can include every type of boat imaginable from a gondola to a barge to a tiny rowboat. Swimming objects outside the booms might include the queen's swans and other waterfowl and the occasional Labrador retriever in pursuit of both.

On Wednesday, June 14, we had our first full day of practice since our arrival in England. In order to avoid colliding with the dozens of other shells on the river, protocol held that you rowed downstream outside the booms, then upstream inside the booms on the course. Notwithstanding

---

* A repechage is a heat where the "fastest" losers of preliminary heats compete for a spot in the final.

the arrival of some 1,000 oarsmen over the next two weeks, the course never seemed crowded. At times it was as if we had the river to ourselves, though a sense of tranquility could be shattered at any moment with the blaring of rock music from Henley's PA system, in sharp contrast to the quiet gentility that was to assert itself during the regatta. A newly minted hit that later came to be a staple at National Hockey League games, Gary Glitter's "Rock and Roll Part 2" seemed to be continually in play, its tempo perhaps an inspiration to the athletes on the water.[*]

If we were suffering from jet lag or just feeling rusty, it didn't show. In the morning practice our times from the start to Fawley and from Fawley to the finish were competitive, a combined 6:50 for the course. The afternoon practice was equally as good, despite rowing at a low twenty-nine. We later went out for a short evening row and did a "Barrier piece"—from the start to the marker known as the Barrier, a little over a quarter mile—and were even faster than we had been in the earlier practices. "Beautiful," Roger noted before turning in that evening.

The Henley course presented a distinct challenge for Roger, so he no doubt welcomed the fortnight of practices as much as we did. Although straight as a gun barrel, the course's width of eighty feet left little room for error. Because the length of an oar is about twelve and a half feet, that meant that about fifty feet of that width was taken up

---

[*] Sports trivia buffs often claim that the song was first wedded to a sporting event at a Colorado Rockies hockey game in the late 1970s. Not so. That honor belongs to Henley.

by the sweeps of the competing boats alone. Ten feet from boom to oar and from oar to opposing oar doesn't leave much room to play with. Many an inexperienced coxswain has crashed into the booms, often costing their crews a race. Furthermore, crews that are leading by open water are subject to disqualification if they move to the middle of the river or otherwise block the opposing boat. (This is not cycling or roller derby.) The only exception is if a crew is so far ahead that it can't possibly block the other crew by taking the middle of the river.

Without another boat beside us, it would be difficult for Roger to practice his spacing between a competing boat and the booms. Some competition finally arrived on Sunday, June 18, in the form of the Bryanston crew we had beaten

Pounding to the finish in practice at Henley. *Author's Collection.*

back in April. With several months of rowing now under their belts, they clearly thought they could take us. But we were a much better crew as well, and in four sets of thirty strokes each we beat them by a length each time.

The following day we rowed down to the scenic village of Marlowe, Buckinghamshire, about six miles from Henley. Meant as more of a pleasure cruise than a practice, we rowed through six of Marlow's famous locks, an experience enjoyed by all except Roger, who continuously had to call for touch strokes to keep us from colliding with the sides of the locks. The Marlow excursion also exposed some tension that had been building in the boat as the regatta drew closer. Stopping for a quick sandwich on the banks of the Thames, we climbed a small knoll that had recently been visited by a number of the queen's swans, one of which had left behind a beautiful white feather about a foot long that I thought would look good, a la Robin Hood, sprouting from John Rooney's ski cap. But Charlie Kershaw was in a mischievous mood and decided that this would be a good time to play keep-away with the most hot-tempered man on the boat. Not unexpectedly, Rooney blew, and Murray had to step in to prevent a battle royal between a wrestler and a hard-hitting hockey player, ultimately neutralizing the situation by tossing the feather in the Thames. Sensing a small victory, Kershaw flaunted the situation with a smirk. Rooney continued to seethe.

We took it out on a Jesus College, Cambridge, eight that had been minding its own business just below the Hen-

We really didn't know how bad the situation was with Geoff until after church the following day. Assembling under a tent at the Leander Club, the Boss delivered the somber news that Geoff, now in hospital and strapped to an EKG, was suffering from a virus that was causing irregularities in his heart. He was definitely a scratch for Henley. He was all smiles when we visited him later, but he must have been bitterly disappointed, unable to fulfill the dream that, until this moment, had been so wonderfully divined on the wall of a shack on an island in Maine. Years later, perhaps long over the disappointment and with the benefit of perspective, he provided me with this account of what happened during the race with Eton.

Charlie has a partial crab before the end of the island. Eton is fast. I look over and see their stroke even with me. We catch up, then after the mile mark my body starts to give out—an English cold, antihistamine that morning, heart rate up, breathless, can't get a full stroke, can't get up the slide the whole way, holding on to the end. We lost. Shit. Heart won't slow down, legs wobbly, eyes seeing vivid colors of blue on the tents, can hardly hold on to the oar, biting the oar at the end of the race. Something is wrong. Hospital. Cardiac ward. Old men, crying little boys because daddy is dying. Empty beds. Staff Nurse Goodchild, my nurse. Husband a rugby player. Pretty brunette—blue eyes.

Waking up in the middle of the night and all the nurses are around my bed having a break. Started to think about a greater race, the race for survival. Changed my life.

"The images and memories from 1972 remain," Geoff concluded, "some joyful, some painful."

After Hart met with us, I momentarily thought that we were at the end of the line for the 1972 Kent crew, that our good fortune had come to an end. But he did what all good coaches do and played the hand he had been dealt. Our spare, Garth Griffin, was a port oarsman and the seat that needed to be filled was starboard. Here, Murray's insistence over the previous winter that Clint Whistler learn to row both port and starboard paid off. Clint was moved to five, Rooney took over at six, and Garth took his place at four. Adding Garth also meant adding about twenty pounds to the boat, but this was probably offset by his fine "blade." Still, the only exercise he had gotten over the previous four weeks was on a bicycle, so he had to get back into rowing shape quickly. We were just three days away from the opening of the regatta.

Murray appealed to Garth to "just stay up" with the rest of us, and after the first practice with the new configuration it was clear that he would do that and more. Although the boat felt different, it didn't necessarily feel much worse. Roger was encouraged, and our times to the Barrier and to Fawley were solid. We went out three times on Monday,

June 26. The morning practice was mixed; the afternoon, better; and the evening session found us "moving very well." The following day we practiced with Harvard in the morning, falling two seconds behind them on a quarter-mile piece, then overtaking them on a shorter piece toward the finish. In the afternoon session we concluded our last full day of practice by taking Bedford University in two short pieces.

The 1972 Henley Royal Regatta opened on Wednesday, June 28. Roger referred to it as the "1930s relived," but he had his King Edwards confused, for when writers and other commentators refer to the Henley atmosphere as Edwardian, they mean not the abdicator but rather the king who reigned over the British Empire during the first decade of the twentieth century. It was kind of a twilight era, one of distinct class division and huge inequities in wealth—all of which would be partially leveled by emerging social movements and the devastating effect of World War I on English society. According to one account the Edwardian Era is nostalgically recalled as "a romantic Golden Age of long summer afternoons, garden parties, and big hats."

We could enjoy the first day of the regatta because all three of the foreign entrants to the Princess Elizabeth Cup had earned a first-round bye, as had our Harvard brothers in the Thames Challenge Cup. Up until 1969 Henley pairings had been quaintly arranged through a random draw held at the town hall the Saturday before the regatta, where the Stewards would "take pieces of paper out of the Grand

Murray Beach, Garth Griffin, Charlie Kershaw, Fred Elliott, John Rooney, and Charlie Poole at Henley. Note the white bucks, de rigueur at Henley. *Courtesy of Fred Elliott*

Challenge Cup beneath portraits of George I and the Earl of Macclesfield," in the words of Henley historian Christopher Dodd. This system proved to be flawed when the best crews all ended up in one half of the draw, however, and apparently this happened often enough that beginning in 1969 the Stewards made an effort to keep the best crews away from each other until the semifinals. The selection was based on merit, so our undefeated record and national championship had earned us our bye. On the other side of

the bracket stood the Canadian national champions, Brentwood College School of Vancouver, and Ridley College of
St. Catherines, Ontario.

Of the eleven entrants to the Princess Elizabeth Cup,
four were thought to be in the hunt to take the prize: Kent,
Brentwood, Ridley, and the 1971 winner of the cup, Pangbourne College, Reading, Berks County. While we didn't
practice with any of the crews, we knew something about
Pangbourne and Ridley from observation, reputation, and
how they had fared against boats that we had rowed with.
Ridley, a perennial Canadian powerhouse that had won the
cup in 1970, had been beaten in practice by both Bedford
and Harvard in short pieces, so we had a feeling that we
had a chance against them. (Indeed, many were looking forward to a Kent-Ridley final.) Pangbourne was small but had
a fast start and a chip on its shoulder as the previous year's
winner. Brentwood was a complete mystery to us and had
in fact just arrived at Henley on Wednesday of the regatta.

Friends and family had assembled as well. My family's
entourage consisted of my parents, Liz, my brother, and
his friend Andy Behar. (The two fifteen-year-olds kept an
especially sharp eye out for abandoned, half-full Pimm's
Cups or champagne to quickly knock down when no one
was looking.) Sid Towle and his wife, Nancy, were there, of
course, as were a number of Kent alums: Tully Vaughan and
his wife; Dick Schell, who had taken a year away from Harvard to study in England; and Thad Bennett, coxswain of
the 1971 crew. Peter Conze, '61, had arrived earlier to assist

with the coaching and provide a little encouragement. He had rowed with KSBC for two years and had never lost a race in the United States

By all accounts my father was in his element at Henley. Not only were the drinks flowing freely, but in the English he had a fresh new audience for his charms. He and my mother immediately befriended the couple my family was staying with, the Simondsons, and Liz played the role of dutiful would-be daughter well. Whatever mischievous things my brother and Andy were up to were generally ignored.

With the festive atmosphere and many alcoholic and epicurean distractions, it almost seemed as though the regatta was a sideshow, but for us the early heats in the Princess Elizabeth Cup were the main attraction that Wednesday. Particularly, a race that afternoon between Pangbourne and another English school, Emanuel, would determine who our opponent would be the next day. As it turned out, it wasn't much of a contest. The clearly superior Pangbourne led at the Barrier by a length and a quarter, two lengths at Fawley, and crossed the finish almost four lengths ahead of Emanuel. As the only crew thought to have a chance to keep the cup in English hands, Pangbourne became a crowd favorite, and for the next twenty-four hours anyway, we would be out of favor with our otherwise cordial hosts.

The start for the Henley course is just beneath Temple Island, a place so named for its magnificent erstwhile fishing lodge, whose interior was based on designs that had been discovered in the ruins of Pompeii. Built in 1771, it became a place for members of the Leander Club to view racing during the Victorian era. (In 1987 the Henley Stewards secured a 999-year lease for the island and set about restoring the Temple. Today it is made available for special events.) For the oarsman it is a landmark *evanidus*, a vanishing point by which to measure progress down the river. Because the Thames at Temple Island divides the counties of Buckinghamshire and Berkshire, the two lanes of the Henley course are named Berks (lane number one) and Bucks (lane number two). And since a scull is much shorter in length than an eight, starting floats can be adjusted so that bows can be visually aligned to be certain that each boat travels exactly one mile, 555 yards.

For our race with Pangbourne on Thursday, June 29, we drew Berks, although there was no particular advantage to being in either lane. We had already watched Brentwood crush our old friends at Bryanston by three and three quarter lengths earlier in the day, but we tried not to make that a distraction as we pulled up to the start floats with Pangbourne at a little after 3:00 p.m. I don't recall anyone being particularly nervous about Pangbourne; we had gone out for a light evening paddle after the regatta had ended the previous day, and it had felt pretty good. We were ready. We had also developed a new rapid full-slide start that seemed to be working well for us.

We went off the line at a forty-four, and immediately someone on the Pangbourne boat caught a crab. The crew regained composure quickly though, and was down by no more than half a length at the quarter mile. We blazed through the barrier in under two minutes, picking up another seat or two on Pangbourne. By the time we reached Fawley we were at a strong thirty-four and had pushed the lead to a length. At this point a roar started to build in the partisan crowd in the grandstands and enclosures as the announcer soberly noted Pangbourne's position. (Because of trees, buildings, and other obstructions, it is not possible to see the entire course from the banks of the Thames near the finish. The announcer's intentionally matter-of-fact delivery is all these spectators have to go by.) Though we had picked up another half-length on Pangbourne at the one-and-one-eighth-mile marker, the crowd begged its beloved English boys to pull

One and a half lengths over Pangbourne. *Author's Collection.*

off a miracle. At that moment we were probably the most unpopular people in all of England. We stayed at thirty-four through the finish, eschewing a sprint out of respect for the fine Pangbourne crew. They were visibly disappointed that they had failed to keep the cup, but being Englishmen, they were gracious in defeat.

Ridley came up the river about a half hour later comfortably ahead of its opponent, King's School, Chester. Its barrier and Fawley times were just above ours, but they had finished strong, winning by three and a half lengths. The following day it would square off against its great rival Brentwood in the semifinal. We would face off against Kings School, Worcester, another small crew averaging just under 160 pounds per man. (By contrast, Ridley averaged nearly 190 pounds and Brentwood close to 180.)

On Friday, June 30, we once again lined up in Berks at the start floats at a little after 3:00 p.m. At the start we moved out easily on Kings and had settled to a thirty-two by the Barrier. And that's where we stayed for the remainder of the race. Even at that relatively low rate we continually gained on Kings, and even though the crowd politely applauded their effort with the occasional "Well rowed, Worcester," there was not the same enthusiasm that there had been for Pangbourne. England's last chance at keeping the Princess Elizabeth Cup was down by nearly seven lengths as we approached the grandstands, though in the spirit of good sportsmanship, judges stop counting lengths at this point and simply determined that we were ahead "easily." (In fact, those who work the scoreboard at Henley anticipate that some races will turn out this way and hoist a sign that says EASILY opposite the winning crew's time.)

If there was any controversy surrounding the race, it might have been that Roger chose to take the middle of the river just after Fawley. Although this is grounds for disqualification, it's the race umpire's call. Roger certainly wasn't able to ask permission, since the umpire's launch is always behind the trailing boat. So it was a bit of a gamble on Roger's part, and could have been viewed as unsportsmanlike as well. On the other hand, disqualifying us at this point would have set up a miserably one-sided final.

A real controversy—one that caused the Stewards to make a significant change to the regatta's sacred rules—erupted earlier in the semifinal race between Ridley and Brentwood. Well ahead of Brentwood "within hail of the finish," as one English commentator wrote, the Ridley number three man's swivel suddenly broke, sending him into the Thames. Since the rules clearly stated that "the whole distance must be completed by the full crew before a competitor can be held to have won a race," Ridley was disqualified.[*]

The disqualification had not only been a severe disappointment for Ridley, but for us as well. We had been fully expecting to face Ridley in the final, and even with Kings School, Worcester, in front of us, we were already look-

---

[*] The rules were changed the following year to bring them into accord with the FISA code that a winner was a winner regardless of how many men or women finished the race.

ing past that race toward Ridley. Though Brentwood had won a national championship, they might not have been the best crew out of Canada by the time Henley came up. (Brentwood had also arrived at the last minute after a long flight from Vancouver, which might have affected its performance in its first two races at Henley.) In an ideal world we would not have lost Geoff, Ridley would never have been disqualified, and we'd be in a hell of a race to determine the best in North America. But it was not to work out that way. Ridley's disqualification had definitely taken some wind out of our sails.

Still, Garth was filling in brilliantly, we had taken Pangbourne out of the competition, and we were the first Kent boat to reach a final at Henley in many years. If our focus had been shaken then we still had an accomplishment to go into the final with: Out of all the competitions for eights— Grand, Ladies Plate, Thames Challenge Cup, and Princess Elizabeth Cup—our time over the course, in the race with Pangbourne, had been the fifth-best so far at 7:09. Brentwood had to this point rowed unspectacularly with a 7:32 in its first race and a 7:39 against the man-down Ridley. It seemed that the Princess Elizabeth Cup was ours to lose.

In the meantime, the Harvard crew led by Al Shealy and Ed Woodhouse had stubbornly made its way to the semifinal of the Thames Challenge Cup, decisively beating English club crews in its first two heats. But a daunting challenge faced them on Saturday: a semifinal with London Rowing Club in the morning and, if successful, the final just five hours later. In the unlikely event that Harvard got past the semifinal—odds makers heavily favored the London boat—the final would be with either Thames Tradesmen or Kingston rowing clubs, far more experienced crews who claimed the river near Henley as their home waters.

Saturday, July 1, broke partly cloudy and cool. The finals at Henley would start at a leisurely 11:00 a.m., but once again we would have to wait until after 3:00 p.m. for our race. I can only speak for my state of mind that day—uncomfortable, out of sync, and a little tired after two consecutive days of racing. Just before noon we were temporarily lifted by Harvard's surprising defeat of the London Rowing Club by one and a half lengths and advancement to the Thames Challenge Cup final, but also felt some pressure to match Harvard's success with a little of our own. The hours leading up to our race were otherwise unpleasant and anxious. I purposely avoided Liz and my parents so as not to subject them to my gloom.

At a little before 3:00 p.m. we took to the water. Just prior to pushing off, Sid Towle had spoken to each one of us. "Mr. Rooney," he told John, "today you are going to put Cochituate, Massachusetts, on the map." As we headed toward Temple Island, a tomblike silence surrounded the boat, the usual nerves now leavened with looming melancholy. Whatever the outcome, this would be our last row together, and though I didn't know it at the time, following this day I would be saying good-bye to at least one of my rowing companions forever. Whether or not our mood affected our performance, the boat felt strong if not particularly sharp as we warmed up.

For its part, Brentwood probably felt fortunate just to have advanced to the final, though somewhat by default. In a magnanimous gesture Ridley let Brentwood use its far superior shell, presumably with its swivel now repaired.

There were a couple of things different about this race from the previous heats. For one thing, Hart would not be in a launch but rather following the race on a bicycle along the towpath where he could better see how we were doing. The Henley finals were also televised, with commentary provided by "Kell" Kelly, the man who had exacted revenge for his father's rejection by the Stewards in 1920. One thing that did not change was the whereabouts of Charlie Poole's mother as we backed up to the stake floats. "I couldn't bear to watch the Kent boat compete," she recalls. For all three races she fled to a "sturdy oak near the finish line which obscured all and any view of the lanes of the two competing shells. My husband was furious with me, but I just couldn't watch."

We had a nice, clean, fast start and moved out about five feet on Brentwood. We were still leading at the Barrier, but not gaining. Whether it was the magic of the Ridley boat, or the fact that Brentwood had now been in England for four days and was thus over its jet lag, the Canadian crew was tenaciously hanging on. As we approached Fawley, Brentwood started to move back on us until the dour race announcer intoned, "At Fawley, the crews are *level*." An audible gasp could be heard from the enclosures. We took leg drives and moved out on them again. They responded similarly and were even with us again. At the mile we were back up, but by just a few feet. And Hart Perry was no longer able to urge us on. He had fallen off his bicycle right after Fawley, and by the time he had gotten back up, the race had passed him by. He never did see the finish.

Much to their credit, Brentwood was giving us everything they had. Fortunately, we were able to match them stroke for stroke to keep the race even going into our sprint to the finish. There, we finally got them for good. The bow

Overtaking Brentwood College School in the final for the Princess Elizabeth Cup. *Author's Collection.*

of the *Sill* suddenly surged forward five feet, a distance that was ultimately the margin of victory. (Since that's roughly the length of the bow deck, which is actually canvas, such wins are said to be "by a canvas." And yes, the Henley scoreboard operators had a placard for that, too.) After we crossed the line there were no high fives, no slaps on the back, no war whoops. We were exhausted. And well we should have been: We had rowed the course in 7:02, the fastest time for any entrant in the Princess Elizabeth Cup that year.

Once we were docked I was met immediately by my parents. My father knelt down to shake my hand and,

Hart Perry guiding the *Sill* back to the boat tent at Henley. The smile on his face says it all. *Courtesy of Fred Elliott*

speechless, looked at me as if he was trying to reach deep into my soul to reclaim something he had lost. After a few seconds he regained his composure and graciously yielded the dock to my mother and Liz. Out of the corner of my eye I saw him walking toward the Leander Club as if in a slow dissolve, his signature stride, as ever, a silhouette of Fred Astaire. I was never to have that sort of moment with him again.

———

In a laugher of a race, Harvard had beaten Kingston Rowing Club by over five lengths, or in the Henleyesque euphemism, easily, to take the Thames Challenge Cup. Kent and Harvard were ultimately the only American crews to bring home trophies, Northeastern University having barely lost to a club from Moscow in the Grand.

The award ceremony was held at 6:15 that evening just as the sun emerged from beneath a dark cloud that had parked itself over the English countryside, looking for all the world like some mysterious alien monolith. For once, the presenter of the trophies and medals would not be the wife of a politician or royalty from some tiny principality but a real athlete, a national hero who had helped lift his country out of its doldrums in the aftermath of World War II. On May 6, 1954, Roger Bannister became the first human being to run a mile in under four minutes, atoning for his dismal performance at the Helsinki Olympics two

The author receiving his Henley medal from Dr. (and later Sir) Roger Bannister, the first human being to run a mile in under four minutes. Roger Stewart is on the steps behind me. *Photo by Stephen G. Rinehart*

years earlier. It was an honor to be shaking his hand, and for an instant while in that grasp I felt the connection from one athlete to another, as if Bannister was saying, "Cherish this."

It didn't take long after the ceremony for several bottles of champagne to be emptied into the Princess Elizabeth Cup, and, while most of the polite company at the Leander Club scooped glassfuls from it, a number of us just tilted the cup back and let the bubbly run down our throats. Liz also presented a pack of cigarettes to me, my yearlong suspension of that bad habit now officially over. Our farewell

Two Elizabeths after the awards ceremony: In this photo with Liz I am clutching the top of the Princess Elizabeth Challenge Cup. *Author's Collection.*

dinner was at the Compleat Angler in Marlow, a dockside inn accessible by both car and boat. At one point toward the end of the evening, Tully Vaughan rose ceremoniously, buttoned his Henley blazer, and marched toward the French doors that opened out to the dock. Shoulders squared, without breaking stride he walked right off the dock and plunged into the Thames.

From early practice at Kent in March to our final at Henley on July 1; we had rowed some 760 miles, the

Best of friends: Hart Perry and Tully Vaughan celebrating our victory at the Leander Club. *Courtesy of Fred Elliott*

equivalent of a journey from New York City to Jacksonville, Florida; had pulled over 43,000 power strokes; and astonishingly, never had to look over our shoulders to find the competition after crossing the finish line. Shortly after Henley, Hart wrote us each a letter where he admitted, "I'm sure there will never be another season like this." Twenty-five years later that sentiment still held, when he wrote, "How vivid are the memories of KSBC '72 at Henley and the bridge we crossed to realize Kent's finest rowing season."

AFTERMATH

"Be thou faithful unto death and I will give thee a crown of life."

—Revelation 2:10

Following Henley we dispersed. The underclassmen of course returned to Kent; Charlie Poole captained the crew the following year, Clint Whistler the year after that. In the summer of 1973, the 1972 Kent crew came together again under the most heartbreaking of circumstances—a staggering blow that had me recalling that mysterious black cloud that hovered over Henley at the award ceremony: Charlie Kershaw was dead, killed in an accident by a drunk driver. The service for Charlie was held at St. Josephs Chapel at Kent; he was later buried in his Henley blazer. I found it unfathomable that the man who had rowed in front of me for four months was now gone. Sadly, that was not the end of our losses. Twenty years later Clint Whistler was found dead under mysterious circumstances. Later, Hart confirmed that it was probably suicide. He apparently had been depressed over the death of his mother and the course of his life in general. The last time I saw him was at a reunion at Kent in 1992. Disturbingly, he was already drinking at nine in the morning that day. We should have seen it coming.

The rest of us survive. Several members of the 1972 Kent crew went on to successful rowing careers at college and afterward. Murray rowed for Harvard and later coached U.S. junior national teams; Fred Elliott's and Garth Griffin's freshman crew at Marietta went undefeated and won the Dad Vail regatta in 1973; and Charlie Poole became the first American oarsman to win at Henley as both a schoolboy and a collegian, winning the Thames Challenge Cup in 1977 with a Trinity College crew of which he was also captain. Roger and Geoff were asked to join the crew program at Princeton, but both politely declined. Geoff, especially, had had enough. John Rooney developed a bad back in 1973 and decided to save his body for hockey. He still plays internationally in senior leagues, and plans on doing so until well into his seventies.

I went away to a college that didn't offer rowing, and except for a brief spell when I owned a single scull, I could justifiably be called an interloper to the sport. Fred, Charlie, and Murray still row in popular regattas such as the Head of the Charles,* and Fred's charming home in Darien, Connecticut, sits on an inlet to the Long Island Sound from which he can quietly paddle out in the evening sun and recall the time his father first taught him to row as a little boy.

Hart Perry's career was straight up from 1972. In 1974 he became the first American to be voted a Steward of the

* Of which the great Fred Schoch, Kent '69, is the current executive director.

Henley Royal Regatta. He won at Henley again in 1979, coaching a Magdalen College, Cambridge, crew in the Thames Challenge Cup, and had another Cambridge crew in the finals in 1986. Five trophies and five boats have been named for him, most recently a Kent eight. He has been inducted into four athletic halls of fame, and in 2009 he and his wife, Gillian, received U.S. Rowing's highest honor, the U.S. Rowing Medal, "given to a member of the rowing community in the U.S. who has rendered conspicuous service to or accomplished extraordinary feats in rowing." Today, Hart serves as trustee and executive director of the National Rowing Foundation, chairs the selection committee of the Rowing Hall of Fame, and coaches at the Coast Guard Academy.

Over the years a few more honors followed for the entire crew. In 1973 we were all voted into membership at the Leander Club in Henley. In 2002 we were inducted into the Kent School Athletic Hall of Fame; John Rooney made it in again for his prowess on the hockey rink a few years later. In 2007 *Rowing* ranked the top-ten "great" schoolboy eights of all time and ranked the 1972 Kent crew third. The greatest honor we received, though, was the retirement and subsequent preservation of the *Sill* shortly after 1972. It hangs today from the ceiling of the second floor of the new Kent Rowing Center.

The decades have brought some resettling to the family as well. My parents divorced after we children were grown and gone and re-paired up with simply wonderful people who enriched their lives and ours. My father quit drinking and smoking in his fifties and at last found his calling helping people through their own drug and alcohol addictions. In the last years of his life, I enjoyed many cordial visits with him and my stepmother, Anne, especially when Dad was in a mood to crank out a colorful, and probably apocryphal, story. And he was always interested in any news of Hart Perry, such was his admiration for him for helping guide his son into manhood. Speaking at Dad's memorial service in June 2007, I tried to recall that moment on the dock after the final at Henley, but then stopped myself, knowing that there were only two people who would ever understand what that was really all about. The moment is secure in the amber of my memory, and there it will comfortably stay as my father still makes the occasional visit to my dreams.

Regrettably, Liz and I were not to be, and went our separate ways after a year at Kenyon. We remain great friends, however, and the years have enabled us both to look back fondly on what was, at times, a truly enchanting period in our lives.

Kent School experienced its own makeover following Sid Towle's death in 1980 after a long illness. Seeing that a drastic change had to be made to ensure the school's survival, the board of trustees took a gamble and elevated thirty-year-old Father Richardson W. Schell, '69, from chaplain to headmaster in 1981. Dick undertook the school's most significant transformation since Father Sill's campaign for the permanent Kent in the 1930s. He first attacked the school's dismal financial situation by bringing it into the black operationally within three years. Realizing that the two campuses would have to be consolidated for the school to be able to carry on, he raised $65 million through loans and gifts and undertook a six-year program of construction to expand the boys' campus to accommodate girls. Between 1998 and 2005 Father Schell led a new Campaign for the Permanent Kent, with a goal of raising $75 million for endowed faculty chairs and scholarship aid. He raised $80.1 million. By its one-hundredth anniversary in 2006, Kent was at last secure financially and was able to keep up with the technological challenges of the twenty-first century. Still, by honoring the original vision for Kent by having its new construction mimic that of the first plan for the permanent Kent, I like to think that Father Sill would have had no problem recognizing today's school.

The sport of rowing, particularly at the high school level, has also gone through a significant transformation since 1972. Kent added girls' crew in 1973, which quickly became swept up in the Kent School Boat Club reputation for excellence. The Kent Girls Boat Club made its first trip to England in 2002 and won at both the Reading and the Henley Women's regattas. The situation for the boys is much changed since my day at Kent. Importantly, the sport is much more competitive at the high school level than it had been in 1972, so there is no longer much need to pad the schedule with the odd college freshman or lightweight boat. Of course, crews are also much faster now and the equipment far superior to what we rowed with. Kent also abandoned the club system for rowing when the emergence of other sports thinned the field of available oarsmen. Today, Kent rowing consists of four boats under the auspices of the Kent School Boat Club.

Kent has not won at the Henley Royal Regatta since 1972, but as of this writing, its 2010 first boat, with its first national championship since 1980 and only one loss, is poised to make the first serious bid for the Princess Elizabeth Cup in thirty-eight years. Still, we are a little like the undefeated 1972 Miami Dolphins, always wishing Kent crews well, but sometimes secretly hoping for our pristine record to stay intact. It won't last—nothing ever does—but it would be nice if the next undefeated season could wait until after we're all gone.

The "flash of red" that I had seen in the display case during my first visit to the rowing center at Kent was John Rooney's red ski cap, my touchstone to the past and the icon from 1972 that started a process that led to the writing of this book. Oddly, something my sister had told me a few years before came to me as my eyes froze on to the display case: "When something happens to you that you didn't expect or felt you deserved, that's called grace." And once again I was hurtled into the mysteries of life with a list of unanswerable questions for God, starting with, *Why me? Why then?* The United States beat the Soviet Union in hockey at the 1980 Olympics at the time of the Soviets' brazen invasion of Afghanistan; the impossible victory was poetic justice. Were the same forces at work in 1972, the fiftieth anniversary of rowing at Kent in which we manned a boat christened the *Frederick Herbert Sill*? I will die not knowing. And yet—whether it is superstition or just covering my bets in a Pascalian way—in my infrequent visits to Kent I make it a point to stop at the small graveyard behind St. Joseph's and, touching the simple oak cross that marks Father Sill's grave, whisper, "Thanks."

As I finish this it is now late spring. As is all too typical of this time of year in Colorado, a cold front has swept through the state overnight bringing lashing rain, fierce wind, cold temperatures, and snow to the nearby mountains. By morning it has cleared, but the wind and the cold remain. As I go outside to observe my wife mournfully cleaning up the damage to the garden, the atmospheric conditions remind me of the race at Derby so long ago, that great test of our will that established what kind of crew we would be for the rest of the season and beyond. Out of the corner of my eye I see a flower bed that has been flattened by the storm and walk over to it to assess the damage. I pull out a flower that has lost all but one petal and let it spin between my fingers as I examine it. As if in an act of mercy, I pull out the last petal and release it into the wind. For a while it spins and turns as if caught in a small cyclone, then a gust of wind off the Rockies suddenly grabs it and blows it eastward, toward New England.

Ready, row.

Courtesy of Kent School

APPENDIX: GLOSSARY OF ROWING TERMS

Backstop: The stop mechanism on the seat slides that prevents the rower's seat from falling off the sliding tracks at the back end (toward the boat's bow) of the slide tracks.

Blade: The spoon- or hatchet-shaped end of the oar or sweep.

Bow or bow seat: The oarsman closest to the front or bow of a multiperson shell.

Canvas: The deck of the bow and stern of the boat, which were traditionally made from canvas.

Catch: The part of the stroke at which the oar blade enters the water and the drive begins. Rowers conceptualize the oar blade as catching or grabbing hold of the water.

Collar (or Button): A wide plastic ring placed around the sleeve of an oar. The button stops the oar from slipping through the oarlock.

Coxswain: The oarless crew member who is responsible for steering and race strategy.

Crab: A rowing error where the rower is unable to timely remove or release the oar blade from the water and the oar blade acts as a brake on the boat until it is removed from the water. This results in slowing the boat down. A severe crab can even eject a rower out of the shell or make the boat capsize (unlikely except in small boats). Occasionally, in a severe crab, the oar handle will knock the rower flat and end up behind him/her, in which case it is referred to as an over-the-head crab.

Double scull (2x): A shell for two scullers generally without a coxswain.

Eight (8+): A shell with eight rowers. Always with coxswain because of the size, weight, and speed of the boat.

Engine room: The middle oarsmen in the boat. In an eight-person shell, these are generally seats 5, 6, and 3 and 4 to a lesser degree.

Ergometer (also ergo or erg): An indoor rowing machine.

Foot stretcher (or just stretcher): An adjustable footplate that allows the rower to easily adjust his or her physical position relative to the slide and the oarlock. The footplate can be moved (or stretched) either closer to or farther away from the slide frontstops.

Four (4-) or (4+): A shell with 4 rowers. Coxless (4-) are often referred to as straight fours, and are commonly used by lightweight and elite crews and are raced at the Olympics. In club and school rowing, one more frequently sees a coxed four (4+) which is easier to row, and has a coxswain to steer.

Gimp seat: Seat 3 in an eight-person boat, often regarded as having the least responsibility.

"Give her ten" (or "Power ten"): A coxswain's common command to a crew to row ten strokes of special effort. It is frequently given when a crew is attempting to pass another boat.

Gunwales (pronounced "gunnels"): The top rail of the shell.

Handle: The part of the oar with which the rowers hold and pull during the stroke.

Hatchet blade: Modern oar blades that have a more rectangular hatchet shape.

Heavyweight: A rower who weighs more than the restrictions for lightweight rowing. Often referred to as open weight.

Launch: A motorboat used by rowing instructors, coaches, or umpires.

"Lay hold" (or "Hands on"): Coxswain's command telling the athletes to go to their stations and grab a hold of the boat.

Leather/Sleeve: A thick piece of leather or plastic around the oar to keep the oar lock from wearing out the wood.

Leg drive: Power applied to the stroke, at the catch, by the force of driving the legs down.

Lightweight: A rower whose weight allows him or her to be eligible to compete in lightweight rowing events. Typically this would mean a crew averaging around 155 pounds with no single oarsmen weighing more than 160 pounds.

Octuple (8x): A shell having 8 rowers with two oars each. Generally a training boat.

"Paddle": Tells a crew to row with just enough pressure to move the boat. The paddle command is also used to bring a crew down from full pressure at the end of a workout piece or race.

Pair (2-) or (2+): A shell with 2 rowers. The coxless pair (2-), often called a straight pair, is a demanding but satisfying boat to master. Coxed pairs (2+) are rarely rowed by most club and school programs.

Port: A sweep rower who rows with the oar on the port, or left, side of the boat.

"Power 10": The command to take 10 strokes at more than full pressure. Used for passing and gaining water in a race. (Sometimes "Power 5," "Power 20," or "Power 30.")

Puddles: Disturbances made by an oar blade pulled through the water. The farther the puddles are pushed past the stern of the boat before each catch, the more "run" the boat is getting.

Quad (4x): A shell having 4 rowers with two oars each. Can be coxed (4x+) or coxless (4x-).

"Ready all, Row": Command to begin rowing.

Rigger: The rowing slang name for an outrigger. It is a projection from the side (gunwale) of a racing shell. The oarlock is attached to the far end of the rigger away from the boat. The rigger allows the racing shell to be narrow, thereby decreasing drag, while at the same time placing the oarlock at a point that optimizes leverage of the oar.

Scull: (a) An oar made to be used in a sculling boat where each rower has two oars, one per hand; (b) A boat (shell) that is propelled using sculling oars; e.g., a "single scull" is a one-person boat where the rower has two oars.

Sculler: A rower who rows with two oars, one in each hand.

Seat: Molded seat mounted on wheels. A secondary meaning is location in the shell (see next entry). Third, it can mean a competitive advantage in a race; to lead a competitor by a seat is to be in front of them by the length of a single rower's section of a shell.

Seat number: A rower's position in the boat counting up from the bow. In an eight, the person closest to the bow of the boat is "bow," the next is 2, followed by 3, 4, 5, 6, 7, and finally 8, or "stroke." In certain countries the seats are numbered the opposite way, from stroke up to bow.

Shell: A boat used for rowing.

Single scull (1x): A shell designed for an individual sculler. Very good for skill development, particularly beginners, and a very competitive class at world events.

Slides (or tracks): Hollow rails upon which a rower or sculler's sliding seat will roll. Older shells might be convex rails with double wheels.

Slings: Folding, portable temporary boat holders. Two are required to hold a boat.

Spacing: Distance between bowman's puddle on one stroke and the point at which the No. 7 rower catches water on the next stroke.

Spoon blade: Traditional U-shaped oar blade (also Macon blade).

Starboard: A sweep rower who rows with the oar on the starboard, or right, side of the boat.

Stroke (seat): The rower closest to the stern of the boat, responsible for the stroke rate and rhythm.

Stroke rate: The number of strokes executed per minute by a crew.

Sweep: A rower who rows with one oar in both hands.

"Weigh enough" (or "Wain...'nuff," or "Way enough"): The command to stop whatever the rower is doing, whether it be walking with the boat overhead or rowing.

ACKNOWLEDGMENTS

If memory serves, I believe it was Fred Elliott who first suggested I write this story some time after the crew broke up after Henley in 1972. For some fraudulent reason I was considered the "poet" of the boat, probably because I had a reputation for remembering a pertinent line of verse when trying to convince a girl that she should waste her time on me. ("Break thy mind to me in broken English, wilt thou have me?" and so forth.) The truth is that for the next twenty years, the most creative thing I wrote was a business plan (several of them), the grocery list representing my most prolific output, and then three books appeared as children sometimes do—eventually. At the conclusion of the third book (cowritten with my wife, Amy), I pulled together a proposal for the present volume and sent it off to my agent, Bob Diforio. Much to my delight, it was quickly accepted for publication by Lyons Press, and I quickly accepted Lyons.

Then came the hard part: reconstructing events that had occurred almost forty years ago with just a few scrapbooks, some photos, and a fading memory to go by. So, in the spirit of being careful with what you wish for, the first person I contacted was Fred. Fortunately, he and his late father, John Elliott, had compiled something of an archive of journals, home movies, and memorabilia of the 1972 Kent crew, which Fred generously shared with me. But Fred's assistance didn't end there: He started to become something of a project coordinator for the book, and helped me hook up with names and faces long gone. More important, sensing that a long silence might mean that I was either stuck or hopelessly adrift in the narrative, he would occasionally drop me a note and ask, "How's it going?" This book belongs to Fred as much as it belongs to me, although I own any errors that may have crept into it.

Our coxswain, Roger Stewart, kindly shared his logs and personal journals with me, which provided me with a road map for much of the narrative. These notebooks—representing fine penmanship and a command of grammar that one came to expect from a Kent student—recall a time when people etched their thoughts in pen or pencil in a gesture toward posterity. Roger chose to donate his logs to Kent in the 1990s, and, seeing their possible value to some future but unknown chronicler, crew coach Eric Houston wisely put them under lock and key until I asked to see them.

Hart Perry, Murray Beach, Charlie Poole, John Rooney, Geoff O'Keefe, Garth Griffin, and Liz Pegram Ralston gave generously of their time responding to e-mails and being subjected to interviews. Of course, I am most grateful for what we accomplished together in 1972. That is their ultimate gift to this book. Victoria Poole, Charlie's "Mum," contributed some wonderful anecdotes that helped bring life to my account of the Henley Royal Regatta.

At Kent School I am grateful to Headmaster Richardson W. Schell and Eric Houston for virtually opening up the place to me for research, as well as for granting permission to reproduce photographs and other archival material. Kent alums Charlie Whitin, Jim Young, Steve Gushee, and Larry Herrick all provided anecdotes about KSBC at Henley.

At Lyons Press the team led by Keith Wallman provided everything a publisher turned fussy author could ask for: professionalism, attentiveness, and encouragement.

Copy editor Chris Jagger and Project Editor David Legere saved me from embarrassing myself with numerous grammatical and typographical contortions, proving that just as a lawyer should never represent himself in court, a publisher should never second-guess his editor.

Finally, I wish to express thanks to four special women whose judgment on preliminary drafts of the manuscript was especially encouraging. Joanne Beattie, chair emeritus of the English department at Kent School, could have politely declined comment but instead chose to run a chapter in the *Kent Quarterly*. My mother, Sharon Caulfield, and my sister, Deb Fowler, encouraged me to "keep going," notwithstanding my rather frank views about our family. My belief is that we all end up in the right place and with the right person eventually, though the path to getting there can be, well, interesting.

The fourth person who helped make this book happen was Amy. The spouses of writers—male or female—are often characterized as people who deliver cookies and tea to the writer at four in the afternoon then quietly disappear. In our household, this is utter nonsense. As a publisher herself, Amy did everything from scan the manuscript for typos to point out potentially embarrassing gaps in the narrative. But Amy's greatest gift to me was that of time—time to write, time away from household responsibilities, and, most challenging for us both, time that we would otherwise be spending together. So thanks, hon. As H. L. Mencken concluded in the preface to one of his memoirs, I've had a lot of fun putting this together.

INDEX

Italicized page references indicate photographs.

ABOUT THE AUTHOR

Rick Rinehart is the author of three books, the most recent of which is *Dare to Survive: Death, Heartbreak, and Survival in the Wild,* co-written with his wife Amy. A member of rowing's prestigious Leander Club in Henley-on-Thames, England, by day Rinehart oversees the trade division of the Rowman and Littlefield Publishing Group. He lives in Lafayette, Colorado with Amy, a yellow lab, and a whippet-pointer-dalmation mix.

Photo by Kay Sorrells